Fault Line

American Lives Series

SERIES EDITOR: Tobias Wolff

FAULT
LINE

Laurie Alberts

University of Nebraska Press • Lincoln and London

∞

Library of Congress
Cataloging-in-Publication Data

Alberts, Laurie.
Fault line / Laurie Alberts.
p. cm. —
(American lives)
ISBN 0-8032-1065-5
(cl.: alk. paper)
1. Alberts, Laurie.
2. Novelists, American
—20th century—
Biography.
3. Alberts, Laurie
—Relations with men.
I. Title.
II. Series.
PS3551.L264 Z466 2004
813'.54—dc21
2003012628

Contents

This is a work of nonfiction. However,
many names and locations have been
changed to protect the privacy of those who knew Kim.

The author wishes to thank
all of those who were willing to share their memories.
Special thanks to Tom and Becky for patience and tolerance.

Fault Line

Prologue

A rancher and his six-year-old daughter, riding fence, found Kim's body. He'd taken off his clothes as he staggered along, strewn them behind him. In his discarded jeans, his wallet held plenty of cash. The temperature was over a hundred the day he died, with a hot wind blowing, but the body lay with knees drawn up, shrunk into a fetal curl. At night, temperatures plummet on the high Wyoming prairie.

He lay out there ten days, not missed, unnoticed, and with the heat and the wind and the animals, there wasn't much left to identify. The little rancher girl will not likely forget that picture: parchment stretched and torn over skeleton. To identify the body, the authorities had to rely on an X ray, taken earlier that year when Kim fell and broke his hip outside a cheap suburban Denver motel. But that was only after they called his brother, Matt, a Pittsford, Colorado, policeman, because the car was registered to Matt's address. Kim had no address of his own.

"I recognized him from the Colorado Rockies cap," Matt said. "I bought that cap for him. We were in a Payless store and he kept picking it up, looking at it, putting it down, and finally I said, 'C'mon, Kim, I'll buy it for you.' He was like a little kid."

Matt is a powerfully built man with light eyes in a tanned face. He competed seriously in rodeos for many years, but roping gave him arthritis in his hands. He intends to retire from the police force in a few years and buy a working ranch.

"I went back to rule out foul play," Matt explained. "I tracked him by the receipts. He had released himself from a hospital with severe dehydration. He was in because he'd been found unconscious in a parking lot in Kimball County, Nebraska. He always carried his fishing and camping gear in his car. He camped near lakes and streams. He'd been to Hawk Springs before. But this time there were monsoon rains and Kim got the car stuck. He'd taken the gate off the dam road and tried to drive across it. There was evidence that he'd struggled to free the car—clothing stuck under the wheels—before he decided to walk out to the road overland. He'd broken his hip in a fall not that long ago and it was still bothering him. He was jaundiced and gaunt. He was only forty-five, but he looked like a seventy-year-old man. He got two miles before collapsing. He only had a mile to go. But he knew what he was doing. He was headed straight for the highway."

A ranch hand astride a small cow pony, moving cattle just outside Hawk Springs State Recreation Area, reported, "I noticed the car but didn't think nothing of it. It was there quite a while. I figured somebody'd gone for help."

The car, a late model Saturn, had belonged to Kim's mother, who had died less than a year before. It held fishing equipment, a sleeping bag, a tent, Gatorade, the bottle of Librium they'd given him for the delirium tremens when he released himself from the hospital. The right number of pills had been taken; Matt counted. Tapes: Simon and Garfunkel, the Beatles—music of the sixties. It also held a small box that he carried wherever he went: his reading glasses, his dead father's watch, notebooks filled with Kim's tiny, even handwriting, a Swiss army knife, and one photograph—a snapshot taken in 1970 at the Cheyenne Mountain Zoo. The young man in the picture wears white jeans, a button-down shirt, and the fatigue jacket he got in ROTC camp. He clamps a pipe between his teeth: a twenty-year-old college boy's affectation. The pipe draws in his already lean cheeks, accentuates his high cheekbones—predicting the gauntness to come but incongruous against the childish cap of blond hair. His eyes look startled, he half turns from one of the animal cages. A bit to the side but in the foreground stands his teenage girlfriend. Her center-parted hair falls straight over her shoulders, black against the pale salmon of her trench coat. Though she is much smaller, she looms in front of the young man, commands attention with the bemused half smile— nearly a smirk—with which she greets the camera. The boy is John Kim Janik, about to begin his senior year at Harvard. The girl in the photograph is me.

See that? I've already turned this story so that I am center stage. I can't help staring into that camera with Kim as my backdrop. It occurs to me that I may not be the most reliable narrator for this tale. How can anyone know if I was at the center of Kim's destruction? But if I don't tell this tale, with all my biases, there is no one else who will. Anyway, it isn't his story but ours.

When I learned of Kim's death, eight months after the fact, I couldn't stop crying. I cried so hard, for so long, that my daughter, not yet three, begged me to stop. "Just think about how nice me and Daddy are to you," she suggested. After two weeks of my unrelenting grief and endless expressions of disbelief—not just that Kim was dead, but that a man in whose strength I still fervently believed could have ended so diminished—my husband grew impatient. After all, I'd had no contact with Kim for ten years. Or so he thought. But he didn't know my secret.

Even now, years after Kim's death, every day, sometimes as many as three, four, ten times, I silently invoke his name. I've done so all my adult life. It is as reflexive as a believer calling out to Jesus, a soldier in a trench crying for his mama. He is my mantra, my shield against humiliation and fear. Kim, I say silently, or sometimes, I need you, Kim. Though I am married, a mother, a woman in her forties. It is possible that his will be the last name on my lips at the moment of my death.

I don't want him to be. I love my husband, my child. Kim is an abstraction, yet unshakable. I have kept him at a distance, but kept him close, too, internal as blood, as threads of tissue, and bone. They say that the lead we consume as children, which our bodies mistake for calcium, stays in our bodies forever, passes from our rushing blood to our skeleton, our silent, grinding teeth. In this way he became part of me, not a poison like heavy metals, exactly, but embedded in the structure that carries me around, allows me to consume the days. Mistaken for nourishment, his is an exacting weight.

I follow my husband, Tom, up the crumbling side of a mesa. His long legs, in blue denim, rise in my view. We have just climbed out of a bowl: red rock above, the soil below us rusty between the dried grasses and cholla cacti. The sky is a silent shriek of blue bedazzled by thunderheads. Here dinosaurs lay down forever, yet half a mile away great earth movers gouge loads of pumice out of the side of White Mesa, grist for stone-washing jeans. Even this prehistoric landscape is precarious.

"I don't get it," I badger Tom. "I just don't see how it could have happened." By "it" I mean Kim's incomprehensible decline. It has been a week since I learned of his death and I can't stop picking at the wound. "That photo," I continue. "He still loved me." The knowledge that he died with a picture of us—of me—in his car, after ten years of separation, is both awful and appealing. Who doesn't want to think herself the object of undying love, the central player in another's drama, even if that drama is questionable?

"Laurie," Tom says, offering me the water bottle. "That picture wasn't about you. It represented his glory days, the high point of his life. It wasn't love, it was obsession."

I'm taken aback. Tom is being uncharacteristically harsh, dismissive of Kim and his love for me. Maybe it's the understandable reluctance of a husband to hear about a former lover. Or the son of an alcoholic's refusal to romanticize that particular destruction. Maybe Tom doesn't want me to self-aggrandize or to presume that I was ever better loved. Obsession, love. Can't they coexist? Does the unhealthiness of one have to cancel out the other?

"You didn't know him," I protest. Though I can't help wondering if I did.

When I learned of Kim's death, I was living in a canyon in the Jemez Mountains, commuting fifty miles to Albuquerque where I taught at the University of New Mexico, shuttling back to Vermont every summer. I'd held this job for nearly six years and had been married just as long. I was always afraid to contact Kim. It would be too distressing for him, I reasoned, for us both. I believed that we would meet again in some indeterminate time when all the wrenching twists of our history would be subsumed by our new lives. In my fantasy, he was sober, perhaps with a family of his own. Why not? If I could settle down, surely he could. Sometimes I pictured introducing him to my curly-headed daughter. We would be tender, rueful, old friends acknowledging the strangeness of having been witnesses to each other's earlier self.

I could not accept this debilitated, desperate Kim. Despite all the evidence, I'd kept an image of Kim formed when I was sixteen, an image I couldn't relinquish. Sure, he drank those last years we were together, but I'd rarely seen him drunk. He'd always functioned. He was articulate, self-possessed. I was furious at every old wino I saw tilting down the Albuquerque sidewalks. *They* got to live to old age. Why hadn't Kim?

My grief wouldn't relent. After two weeks, I turned to a healer, a friend who was studying with a shaman at the Laguna Pueblo. I'm no New Age seeker, and although I admire Margaia, a former nun, I'm sometimes amused by her belonging to the tribe of Anglo "Wannabe"

Indians that flourishes in the Southwest. But I was desperate for a cure, for something to ease this ache. In one part of the ceremony Margaia created for me, she instructed me to picture Kim in a place that had meaning for us both. Lying on the floor of Margaia's adobe house on the side of a mesa in New Mexico, a house my carpenter husband helped to reshape, I entered Lehman Caves in Nevada, where Kim and I stopped in 1970, the summer of that photograph.

We'd been caught in a violent, sudden thunderstorm and because we were nearing a tourist attraction, which promised stalagmites and stalactites, we pulled in. The thunder and lightning might have been on a movie screen, for their sudden disappearance as we went underground. We were the only visitors. Under sizzling lights, we followed a catwalk through enormous caverns and great ballrooms of stone. Deep below the boom of thunder, the great forked spears of lightning, we entered near silence. Just the drip and seep of moisture on the cave walls, our guide's practiced drone. It amazed me to be so suddenly sheltered from the whip of wind, the leaves turning over, the sky breaking apart. An hour later we emerged into the brightness of the world, blinking. The storm was gone, the world washed and glistening, the puddles already evaporating in a western sun that seemed both fickle and thrilling.

Twenty-six years later I conjured Kim a hundred feet below the earth's surface, but he was ahead of me, opening a stone door in the cave wall, his head turned to look back at me while he slipped through. "Come back," I called. But he wouldn't. His face was as closed to me as the door behind which he chose to walk away. He *wanted* to enter that mausoleum, I realized, and I stopped crying.

Later I imagined following him through that doorway, trying to bring him back. "Kim," I would say. "Wait."

"Forget it," he'd answer.

"No, I mean it. I'm sorry."

"Too late for that." But he'd hesitate.

I'd still have absolute confidence in my pull over him. "Let me know you," I'd beg.

"You didn't want to all those years, what's different now?"

Because now I can't have you. I can't call you back. "I don't want you to do this to yourself," I'd say, and that too would be true.

"Do what?"

"Destroy yourself."

"That's my business. And that's your perspective. Maybe I'm enjoying myself."

"I don't believe you."

"I didn't ask you to."

"Kim, can't you . . ."

"See, Laurie, you still want to change me. You never could accept me as I am."

"This isn't who you are!"

"Yes, Laurie, it is."

"No, it was different once. You were open to things."

"I'm open to things, Laurie, just not things that matter to you."

"You don't have to do this, Kim. Kim, if it were different, if we could be together, would you stop?"

"Lau-rie. Don't do this, kid. You don't mean it."

"I don't want to see you go through that door. I don't want you to do this. When you die, I'll cry for weeks."

He turns away, says softly, "I wanted you and I wanted you beyond my grasp."

"Kim," I say, "let's go back. Let's do it again," in my fervor forgetting my husband, my child—"only this time, with what I know now. So I won't have to do those things I did to you. . . . It's you I wanted. I wanted to be with you and rub my mind against yours."

"Your mind, Laurie? Don't you remember the problem was what you were doing with your body?"

"Please, Kim, can I go with you?"

"You don't want to."

"I do. I want to see what draws you, what it's like."

"A quick glimpse into the abyss, eh? A whiff of brimstone and treacle."

"Yeah."

"Remorse is a killer, Laurie."

In the "healing" ceremony, Margaia had me write a letter to Kim relaying what I was sorry for—my many betrayals—and what I was angry about—his refusal to live—and then she burned it and swept the smoke skyward with a raven's wing. I couldn't help wondering where she got that wing. A dead bird by the side of a highway? Or was there a shaman supply store somewhere? In a shell on her coffee table, yel-

RUSH MY
FREE ISSUE!

BUSINESS REPLY MAIL

FIRST-CLASS MAIL   PERMIT NO 515   MARION, OH

POSTAGE WILL BE PAID BY ADDRESSEE

E THE
ENVIRONMENTAL
MAGAZINE

SUBSCRIPTION DEPARTMENT
PO BOX 2047
MARION OH 43306-2147

low lined paper curled to ash but the record of my crimes and accusations didn't dissipate with the smoke that mingled with the purifying sage she lit. I stopped crying, but I wasn't healed of my grief, my anger, or my remorse.

The dreams came next:

April 12, 1996

Kim was big and healthy and handsome again. Drinking. I felt intense desire for him, desire magnified by the knowledge that he'd soon be gone. He took me to a motel—the sink dirty, strange men lounging around. Kim said, "Do you want me to stop drinking?" I said, "No, you'll have the d.t.'s. Can't you stop now and have a drink at 3 A.M. to avert them?" But of course he couldn't. We both knew he was going to die. Before the dream ended, I realized the only solution was for us to commit suicide together.

What am I to make of a dream in which I chose to kill myself in order to stay with Kim, a dream I had the night before my daughter's third birthday? *This* is my real life: the cake I frosted pink because she asked for it, and the gift of a wooden box I glued with chunks of agate and turquoise and tigereye she and I dug behind an abandoned shack once owned by a gem polisher. I added a fossil shell I picked from a limestone cliff, vestige of the great sea that once covered this desert; and a pottery shard, a triangular piece painted with black zigzags, remnant of a vessel an Anasazi hunter may have dropped eight hundred years ago.

Now that we've returned to Vermont for good, my daughter may not remember that we once lived in a land where history keeps surfacing as water erodes soil and volcanic rock. I made her the box as an emblem of when she was three, a time that may someday seem to her as ancient and unknowable as the eons in which that shell was formed, that pottery shaped. As ancient as my time with Kim now seems to me.

Kim's death has done this: washed away what covers memory to reveal the jagged detritus of ruins, and momentary perfections, lovely as frozen trilobites and columnar coral. Our fossil life, our past.

He was the Harvard bartender; I was the hot hors d'oeuvres girl. I'd been hired to carry canapés at a cocktail party held before a gala at the synagogue my family fitfully attended. The hosts lived in a faux colonial in a woodsy development across town. "There's going to be two Harvard juniors," Mrs. Kaplan informed me with a conspiratorial smile as she showed me how to shuttle cheese puffs from a cookie sheet to a silver tray. Her dentist husband always hired bartenders from the student employment agency.

Then two robust boys filled the kitchen doorway with their bumptious energy, their banter trailing in with the cold November air. I quickly dismissed the one Mrs. Kaplan introduced with special emphasis as *Andy Jacobs*; he appeared generically Jewish with his pink skin and kinky hair. The other boy, very tall and blond, was more to my tastes. Mrs. Kaplan mumbled his name.

"Look boys, what a cute helper we've got tonight," she said.

I murmured a self-conscious hello and they went down to the finished basement to don their little red monkey jackets and set up the bar. I wore no uniform beyond the acceptable costume of 1969: a purple minidress over black tights; my center-parted hair straight to my waist. I had outlined my eyes with liner, spread pale color on my lips.

The doorbell rang and the house filled with guests, including my parents. Then I was busy, trotting upstairs to replenish my trays, pushing through the swirls of smoke and chatter, the guffaws and shrills. I asked, "Would you care for some hors d'oeuvres? Would you like a canapé?" I displayed more poise than I normally felt, since I didn't have to make the kind of conversation that would have left me rigid with shyness at the school dances I'd avoided.

As the party wore on and the guests got liquored up, the men, as old as my father, began to answer my scripted questions with lewd suggestions. I snuck a break in an upstairs den. A wall of bookcases displayed hardback best-sellers and leather-bound classics. A decorator's touch, I suspected. At sixteen my intellectual snobbery was already reflexive.

"Anything good in here?"

I turned. The blond boy, whose name I hadn't caught, stood in the doorway. His size struck me first, the height and breadth of him. His sharply angled cheekbones, cleft chin, and thin ascetic lips could have qualified him as a poster boy for the Master Race, but the floppy hair and sprinkling of freckles across his nose put me in mind of an overgrown Huck Finn. He approached the bookshelf, studied it.

"It's just for show," I said. "I bet they haven't read half of them. Well, maybe the Harold Robbins."

He turned to me, grinned. "You got them pegged, huh?"

It was no great accomplishment to peg them. I knew these people; my father read Harold Robbins.

"Here's something good: Auden." He let it flop open, read aloud:

> About suffering they were never wrong,
> The Old Masters: how well they understood
> Its human position; how it takes place
> While someone else is eating or opening a window or
> just walking
>   dully along . . .

"Good stuff!" he said with such enthusiasm that I felt chastened; he was interested in the words, not in skewering our employers' pretensions.

"Oh," I said, pleased to recognize it, "that's the Icarus poem. There's another poem by Constance Carrier about that same painting. We had to write an essay comparing them."

"Which one did you like better?" His blue eyes kindled and his body tensed—a palpable alertness, interest made physical.

"Carrier, I guess. Auden seemed judgmental about the peasants' indifference. I thought she cut them a little slack." Later, I'd be embarrassed to learn that Auden was the better poet.

"You think he was judgmental? I thought he was realistic. Do you know the one by William Carlos Williams, called 'Landscape with the Fall of Icarus?'"

I shook my head. "Is it good?"

"Not as good as Auden. Are you an English major?"

"I'm in eleventh grade."

"You're in high school?"

"Uh-huh." Okay, he could leave now, if he wanted to. I turned back to the bookshelf, where the complete works of Shakespeare stood smooth and stiff. I fingered *The Merchant of Venice*. "I had to play Jessica, Shylock's daughter, in eighth grade," I said. "I wanted to be Portia. I memorized her speech: 'The quality of Mercy is not strained. . . .' Jessica wasn't so bad, though, better than in fifth grade when I had to play Shylock and demand my pound of flesh."

"You put on Shakespeare plays in fifth grade?"

"Uh-huh. Every year. We had to direct them ourselves."

He shook his head. "I can't believe the difference between your school system and mine. We were doing book reports from the encyclopedia in high school."

"Where'd you grow up?" I asked.

"A little town near Boulder, Colorado, called Morrissey."

I'd never been west but pictured the Rockies upright, white-capped, a taller version of the White Mountains where our family went every winter weekend to ski.

"Are *you* an English major?" I asked.

"Soc Rel. That's social relations, psychology, sociology, but lately I've been taking a lot of lit classes and I'm thinking of switching to

English. I started in physics." He slid Auden back on the shelf, leaned against the leather volumes.

"I'll probably major in psychology when I go to college," I said. I couldn't believe that I was standing here conversing with a Harvard junior when I could barely talk to the kids in my grade. But it was easier with him. He talked about what I was familiar with—schoolwork, books. Boys my age boasted and cursed and horsed around, even the geekiest of my AP classmates.

"Really? Clinical or Cognitive?"

I didn't know the difference. "I'm mostly interested in abnormal child development." I'd been swept away by reading *Dibs* and *David and Lisa*. Also by a crush on my psychiatrist, a narrow-shouldered man who resembled Mr. Rogers and who had just last week told me, when I called him up to share what seemed like a pressing insight, that he couldn't be my Saturday night date. The words still burned like a slap.

Mrs. Kaplan peeked into the room meaningfully, withdrew. "I better go hoist some cheese puffs," I said, returning Shakespeare to the shelf.

"Yeah, I got to go back down there and give Andy some help or he'll want to keep all our tips. So, Laurie."

I waited.

"I really enjoyed talking to you. Can I call you so we can continue?"

No one had ever said they liked *talking* to me before. "Okay, but . . . sorry, I didn't catch your name."

"It's Kim."

The name struck me as both exotic and insubstantial. Something skimmed or hummed or hymned. Ambiguous in gender, not quite serious. Eventually I'd learn that Kim was his middle name; his first name was John, as was his father's. I'd wonder what prompted his mother to come up with something so fanciful for her firstborn. Her increasing religiosity accounted for her naming her second son Matthew Paul.

In the Kaplans' den, Kim pulled a tiny Old Mr. Boston Bartender's guide out of his back pocket and wrote my number below a recipe for Brandy Alexanders. He looked up, his blue eyes frank and eager. Then he shook my hand, a firm squeeze, as though sealing a deal.

"Don't get your hopes up," my mother warned that night after returning from the gala. "You're in high school. He's in college. He might forget he even met you."

It wasn't vanity that made me think she was wrong.

Sometimes I wonder if it was Harvard I fell in love with, as much as Kim. For a teenager growing up just seven miles away, hip Harvard Square was the center of the universe, and for AP kids like me, Harvard was the pinnacle, the goal. In Lexington, a town where SAT scores served as currency, we'd been ranked since grade school, segregated from the other students, taught to think of ourselves as superior and entitled. The assumption was that we would be scattered to the nation's best colleges, where we would excel and become the country's leading thinkers, but no place was better than Harvard. Even my father, who drove his Cadillac to his factory in New Hampshire every day and talked about "Taxachusetts commie eggheads," considered my cousins Rona and Robin at Radcliffe to be paragons.

Start with a bird's-eye view, the Charles River with its decorous bridges and boathouses. The crews on the river lean into the weight of their oars, pulling, flexing their strong young calves. The sycamore trees with their patchy white bark form an elegant colonnade along Memorial Drive. Bumpy brick sidewalks lead to Harvard Square, with its high fenced Yard and pompous inscriptions: "Open ye the gates that the righteous nation which keepest the truth may enter in. VE RI TAS." Up Brattle Street, back then, you'd find the club and head shop Truc, the Brattle Street Theater, the Window Shop, where my mother brought me for ladies' lunches, the professors' three-story wooden houses with their elaborate fences and smug charm.

I loved it all: traffic lurching past the news kiosk in the middle of the Square, kamikaze pedestrians shooting out between the cars. On the corner stood the Harvard Coop, aisles jammed with books and posters. At Brighams', people emerged bending over top-heavy ice cream cones speckled with chocolate jimmies. Harvard boys crowded the sidewalks: pimple-faced with green book bags slung over hunched shoulders, or golden WASP athletes sporting a crimson H on their chest. Until Kim, I was just another high school kid traipsing through the Square, sucking up a bit of the vibe, while Hare Krishnas chanted through the streets with their shaved heads, their saffron robes and tambourines.

Kim told me he was disappointed when he first saw Harvard, coming up out of the subway—a screeching hole he'd been terrified to enter. He'd landed alone at Logan Airport, a seventeen-year-old from the West who'd never been on a plane. He'd expected picture book elegance, stone structures commanding a grassy New England knoll, instead of the urban confusion of brick dorms and academic buildings set amidst the honking cars and cheesy luncheonettes. It was the first of his Harvard disappointments.

Kim picked me up in a green-gold Chevy Malibu. His father had bought it for him for his trips back and forth to Colorado. I wondered how his father could afford it, since Kim said he worked in the warehouse of a ski boot company, shifting boxes. "A lumper," my father would have called John Janik. Kim said that a few years ago his father had been promoted to foreman but had asked to be demoted after a day; he couldn't stand the pressure. That lack of ambition was inconceivable to me. I thought everyone wanted to be *more*.

We traveled Route 2 ("Rowt," Kim pronounced with his Colorado accent), past Fresh Pond Circle, to Cambridge, crossing the bridge to Storrow Drive and into Boston. We managed to find a parking space, and in Copley Square Kim put a hand on my back, guiding me gently across the street. In the darkened downtown Boston theater we sat in front of the parents of a girl I knew, and in a moment of panicked introduction I forgot their names.

The movie, *Putney Swope*, mortified me. In one scene an actor sat inside a toilet stall conversing with his pants around his knees; in another, shot in slow motion, bare-breasted beauties jumped into the air, their globelike breasts flying with a fullness I knew I'd never match.

When news of my Harvard date had run through the family, my cousin Sherry, a freshman at BU (or B. Jew, as it was called hereabouts), had phoned to give me advice. "You'll have to sleep with him on the first date," Sherry informed me knowingly. "College boys expect that."

I was terrified, not so much of the sex, which was still an abstraction to me, but of having to get naked in the process. I was sure that, under my clothes, I was a hideous freak. Since eighth grade I'd been starving myself. I'd never been fat and I wasn't actually emaciated now, just right in the age of Twiggy, but thin enough to stop my periods and keep me from growing breasts. I stuffed my bras with Kleenex and feared exposure.

I carried myself as though protecting a secret, but it wasn't just my lack of breasts I was hiding, though I couldn't have said that then.

The secret was the chaos within our neat little colonial reproduction on a historic route in historic Lexington—a house that had, by town decree, to be painted white with black shutters. A house in front of which Paul Revere's celebrated ride was duplicated each Patriot's Day. I held within me the sound of a glass shattering on the kitchen lino-leum, my father's car, engine gunning, chasing us down the driveway, noisy restaurant walkouts, a nighttime trip to the emergency ward, an eighth grade school portrait with a fading black eye, the sight of my father's Adam's apple, its brutal rhythmic bob each morning as he poured cold water into his tea and glugged it down before driving north to New Hampshire, cursing us all. What I hid, of course, was my terror. I was surprised when I learned that some of my classmates in-terpreted my stiff and fearful demeanor as being "stuck up." I didn't feel superior until I had Kim.

After the film, we drove back to Cambridge, hunted the side streets in vain for a parking space, finally parking illegally, which Kim said was his usual habit. He'd already accumulated fifty or so unpaid parking tickets in his glove box; the cops never bothered tracing him back to Colorado. His disdain for the law struck me as bold, if unsettling.

We walked the cold Cambridge sidewalks, amidst students hunched in winter coats, carrying piles of books. "Wonks," Kim called them, explaining that it spelled "know" backward, geeks returning from the library on a Saturday night. The jeering beer-soaked voices of the jocks echoed down the side streets. Kim escorted me into the gat-ed courtyard of Quincy House, past buildings massed in darkness, lit by windows through which I hoped to catch a glimpse of mysterious college life.

Kim and Andy's suite held two bedrooms and a common room com-plete with fireplace, a coffee table holding a bottle of vino fino encased in woven straw, a beat-up couch, an old round-shouldered refrigerator, a stereo, and a long line of albums standing against the wall.

Kim stacked records. The music surprised me, not Led Zeppelin or the Stones, but the light chiming tones of Pentangle. I went into the bathroom. When I flicked on the light, I confronted a marble wall plastered with a collage of *Penthouse* and *Playboy* centerfolds. Enor-mous, pink-nippled breasts filled my line of vision, as if to drive home once again my own deficiency and the inevitability of Cousin Sher-ry's warning.

"That's some wallpaper you've got in there," I tried to joke when I came out.

Kim waved a dismissive hand. "It's Andy's." He opened the refrigerator. "Would you like something to drink?"

Did he mean beer? Wine? I didn't drink. I wouldn't waste calories on a liquid.

"I've got cider."

"No thanks." Internally, I totted up the day's food consumption once again. Safe, for the moment.

Kim closed the refrigerator and bent before the fireplace.

I sat stiff and self-conscious on a rug in front of the fire, my legs crossed, watching the flame take hold of paper, kindling, and logs. Kim turned off the overhead lamp. I cringed. Here it comes, I thought, when he sat beside me, but he kept his attention on the fire.

"Where's Andy?" I asked.

"Working a party."

"Mrs. Kaplan wanted me to hook up with him instead of you," I said.

Kim laughed. "I could tell." Then his voice changed, hardened. "My last girlfriend, Marilyn, broke up with me because she was Jewish and I wasn't." Kim got up to fetch a log from a pile by the entrance. "I'd rather have someone hate me than be indifferent," he said with sudden and surprising bitterness. He positioned the log and sat back down.

I thought it a strange view; indifference sounded better to me than hatred any day. "That whole Jewish thing doesn't mean much to me," I offered. "My parents made me go to Saturday school for eight years, but they don't believe in it. My father only goes to temple on the High Holy Days, and he wears sunglasses and falls asleep and snores and pisses off the rabbi. It's really embarrassing. What were you raised?"

"My mother couldn't make up her mind. She's Lutheran now, but when I was little she kept switching churches."

"So are you a Lutheran too?" I wasn't sure what a Lutheran was, exactly. All the Protestant denominations ran together in my mind.

"Ab-so-lutely not." Kim poked the log and sparks flew up. Then he smiled. "I believe in the rational mind."

At ten-thirty, my anxieties shifted. Kim had to drive me home before my curfew. He hadn't made a move. Did that mean he only liked *talking* to me? Did he find me unattractive, even with my clothes on?

At our house he got out to open the car door for me, then bid me goodbye beneath the bronze eagle nailed to our garage eaves. "I had a nice time, Laurie. I'd like to see you again. Would you like to go skiing with me next weekend?"

"All right." I waited for a goodnight kiss that didn't come, then turned in puzzled embarrassment and hurried up the steps. One thing I knew: Sherry was wrong.

Heading to New Hampshire that weekend, I critically studied my thighs, imagining their spread on the car seat beside Kim's to be too wide. Just the week before I'd been sent to an endocrinologist at the Tufts teaching hospital. "There's nothing wrong with me except I'm too fat," I told the doctor. "Do you want to look like you came from Bergen-Belsen?" he fumed. I'd crossed my arms and fumed back. I knew how disgusting my flesh was. But when Kim and I skied down the ramp from the first chairlift, I judged Kim, not myself.

I was disappointed, embarrassed for him. He skied enthusiastically, fast and wild, but with no form. He kept his skis too far apart, his upper body hunched. My brother and sister and I had been started on rope tows at three, forced to take lessons for years, and kept our skis together in perfect parallel. Kim didn't even have ski clothes; he wore a green fatigue jacket, white jeans. But his equipment was first rate. His father got him boots and skis discounted through his job. I tried to overcome my disappointment at Kim's lack of skiing style. It helped that he seemed fearless, bombing down black diamond slopes with a whoop, his pale cheeks pinked by the cold.

On the way home we stopped at Greeley Park, in Nashua, because I mentioned that I had lived in a house nearby until I was nine. Although there was no snow this far south, it was cold and I suggested we make a fire in one of the stone barbecues. Kim gathered downed pine branches, constructed a Boy Scout's teepee of kindling, and blew until smoke curled up and the boughs ignited. Later he told me he was scared that he couldn't get it going without paper. Having never built a fire, I didn't know it could be hard to start one or that Kim might be nervous about failing in front of me.

We stood before the welcome heat. A mat of dead winter grass spread under well-spaced, huge white pines in a park where twelve years before I'd splashed in a wading pool, eaten bologna sandwiches, and been lifted onto a stone cannon for a snapshot while my father scowled. I could almost see, across the busy road, the beautiful colonial house with the curved staircase and leaded glass windows, a house in which my mother slumped on the couch crying, while I, at four and five and six, listened to her tales of woe and tried to comfort her.

Kim pulled me against him, kissed me for the first time. The cold stiff cloth of his green fatigue jacket, the warmth of his lips, his height as he bent over me, the crackle of burning pine branches—all of it so foreign. What was I doing here with this eager stranger?

"You didn't kiss me after our first date," I said, leaning back to eye him.

"I enjoyed our conversation so much I didn't even think of it."

"I thought maybe you didn't like me, you know, like *that*."

"I like you, Laurie," Kim said, "a lot. You're so pretty and smart, I can't believe I found you."

I wasn't as pretty or smart as he thought I was. I had a freakish body and I went to school with kids who aced double 800s on their SATs. Kim kissed me again, then he held me to his chest. *Pretty, smart*—the praise was enough to turn my head. He was so sweet, so big. I allowed myself to soften. Was this how a child felt in its mother's arms?

My mother instructed me that I shouldn't say yes every time Kim asked me out. I ought to preserve "the mystery." I answered with tremendous assurance that if knowing me was going to be a disappointment, I'd rather he got it over with now. My mother had lost all authority. I knew more than she did, more than my high school acquaintances, more than anyone did. I'd been lifted into some exalted state rarely meted out to high school juniors.

At Quincy House, behind gated brick walls, boys sailed Frisbees and tossed footballs. In F-22, the radiators rattled and groaned, releasing shots of steam. From the turntable issued the trumpety blare of Blood, Sweat, and Tears; Crosby, Stills, and Nash's sweet harmonies; Joni Mitchell's soaring "Ladies of the Canyon"; the Beatles's brazen cheer. Andy's artwork, the *Playboy* and *Penthouse* centerfold collage, had been ripped down by some women who came to a party and liberated the bathroom.

Beside Kim's narrow cot hung a small reproduction of Salvador Dali's *The Persistence of Memory*—an ugly picture, dripping with melting clocks. I didn't understand its appeal to him then, though now it makes too much sense. At Kim's scarred wooden desk we hunched over separate texts. Kim tamped his pipe with a wide-headed nail. Under a sweet haze of Borkum Riff, he read my school papers, and I read his, at least those I could understand. We discussed endlessly, eager to flex our agile minds.

When we needed a break from our studies, we roamed the streets of Cambridge and Boston, taking in dinners at Legal Seafoods, *The African Queen* at the Brattle Street Cinema, *Joe Egg* at the Loeb Theater, The Doors at the Boston Gardens, a Harvard-Yale game in the stadium where the year before Andy and Kim had jobs hawking hot dogs.

In our recent e-mail correspondences Andy Jacobs remembers our Harvard time as joyful and says that I was "a little jewel of fun in those years." I remember my time with Andy differently. He thought Kim should be dating his peers, college upperclassmen, not a high school girl. I didn't think it questionable that Kim was dating a high school girl because *I* was that girl. "Andy's just jealous," Kim said.

If Andy has forgotten our antagonism, maybe I've forgotten too much of the goofy fun. Knowledge of what became of Kim and me later may have colored my perceptions just as nostalgia has smoothed the edges of Andy's recall. Andy reminded me that he and Kim sent a Bible from a freshman humanities course to a girl Kim knew back in Colorado whose fundamentalist parents had sent her to Bob Jones University. They cut out the center of the Bible and filled it with tiny airplane booze nips. They held snowball wars and rolled a three-foot snowball into a friend's dorm room and left it there. And they got free beer for taking part in a survey run by a research company for which Kim had worked. Where did I, the little jewel, fit in? "You were the damsel," Andy said, "we were protecting in the snowball fights."

At night, Kim and I clutched each other in his narrow sprung cot. I traced the T of hair on his chest, down to his navel, and said, with no trace of irony, no awareness that I desired a womb more than a lover, "I wish you had a zipper so I could climb inside. I want to be that close." I didn't realize that most women wanted a man to climb inside them. I needed a mother, a father, and Kim, so much older and wiser at twenty, was willing to be both.

I was still a virgin, though Andy, the night we all met, had bet Kim that I wasn't. (It made me uneasy to think that I'd projected a sexual worldliness that I didn't possess.) Kim didn't pressure me. He was ashamed, he said, that he'd been callous enough to be angry with his high school girlfriend when she missed a period. But now that he was really in love, he said, he saw me as a separate person, not there to meet his needs. We held each other in his bunk, and the yellow light that flooded his room through the bare and discolored shade seemed emblematic of our love. I believed we lived in golden illumination.

In the dark bower of the Harvard Club I stood between Kim and Andy, handing out drinks. "Here, Mr. Mailer, your bourbon," Kim offered smoothly. I'd just finished *Miami and the Siege of Chicago*, on Kim's recommendation, in preparation for Norman Mailer's visit. I watched George Plimpton glad-handing friends. With disappointment I noted that even these distinguished men seemed uncomfortable until they'd had their first and second drinks. I thought social unease was something that adults grew out of. In my fantasy I moved gracefully through a drawing room where brilliant conversations sparkled like the highball glasses at the Harvard Club. I didn't consider Kim's fantasies or where he thought he was headed.

He appeared comfortable with these luminaries, even in a service position. Everyone knew that Harvard Student Bartenders weren't really servants; they were boys on their way to a future. He laughed about seeing John Kenneth Galbraith waffling over the purchase of a Bic pen at the Harvard Coop. He wasn't impressed by names, achievements, although he joked that he was uneasy in the presence of men taller than he.

Kim told me he'd taken a Cliffie, a Cabot from the great Boston family, on a date to Plum Island where they'd ended up throwing paper plates at each other on the beach.

"So why'd you ask her out if you guys didn't like each other?" I grilled him, ready for jealousy over something that had happened before we met.

"Maybe just to see if she'd go out with me."

I wonder now what insecurities—economic, geographic, physical— that comment might have signaled.

"Kim had an innate hostility toward the East," Andy Jacobs remembers. "We both signed into Quincy House. It didn't have the pretentiousness of some of the other houses whose preppy cliquishness Kim took as personally offensive. We were roommates because we weren't part of any group, you know, like when the kickball teams are picked. We were the ones left over. Kim told me that freshman year, after he got all moved into his dorm he went back and sat on the porch and laughed at all the other students moving in."

I picture a seventeen-year-old Kim, who had never been on a plane before and was afraid of the subway, laughing at the well-to-do prep-pie kids unloading station wagons with their parents. But in 1969, my need to believe in Kim's strength kept me convinced of his ease in any surroundings.

Andy says, "Harvard relativism could be described as 'everything you know is wrong so start all over again.' That part really hit Kim hard and . . . is certainly part of his antagonism to the place. I think the op-posite emotion is also generated: a fascination and competitive chal-lenge that runs along the lines of 'I am as good as any of these peo-ple, this place isn't so tough.' The tension between these emotions may take a lifetime to resolve."

How could I doubt Kim's confidence? Kim was smart enough to get A's though he rarely attended classes; he just picked up the as-signments and wrote the papers. I was both disturbed and awed by this. When I sat in on a few of Kim's "Soc-Rel" classes, I found them shockingly dull. In a course on the psychology of love, the professor lectured on the number of turds released by a single rat placed in a cage with a motorized toy Ferrari, versus two rats caged with the toy car. Another psych professor read, without looking up, a deadly lec-ture on Jean Piaget, focusing on the scientific papers on mollusks Piag-et wrote when he was eleven years old.

Our real education came from Kim's reading. I was his willing pupil. I struggled through Pound and Eliot, memorized the lines "The appa-rition of these faces in the crowd / petals on a wet black bough" be-cause Kim praised them. When he told me I reminded him of Prince Andrei's sister in *War and Peace,* I read that too, skipping Tolstoy's philosophical digressions, searching for my doppelgänger. When I got to Prince Andrei's sister I was offended. I'd expected some romantic beauty, not a trembling spinster, devoted to and terrified of her father. How could Kim see me that way, and if he did, how could he love me? I didn't know then that my fearfulness, my great need to be rescued, were as attractive to him as my precocity or my appearance.

Kim adored Yeats, Auden, Faulkner. I read *The Sound and the Fury* because Kim admired it, and begged Quentin Compson, another mis-placed provincial boy in Cambridge, not to commit suicide. I had no idea that within a few years Kim would develop a fixation as hopeless as Quentin Compson's obsession with his sister Caddie's virginity. He would rage over what I would rarely share with him but soon would squander so easily, so infuriatingly, with other men. That first lovely winter, though, our obsessions were simpler. We gobbled up *Light in August* and *As I Lay Dying.* "My mother is a fish," Kim quoted Faulkner.

Kim's mother sent him a Bible called *Good News for Modern Man,* a vernacular Bible stripped of its grandeur in an attempt to sucker more believers. Its line drawings illustrating the parables were equally crude. She also sent a tithing wheel by which Kim could conveniently determine his debt to her church according to his income, with a passage underlined for Kim by her pastor: "What profit a man if he gains the world but loses his soul?"

He told me that when she was a Jehovah's Witness, he'd had to go door to door with her proselytizing, pushing *The Watchtower.* I picture it now: a chubby ten-year-old Kim (improbable as it seems, he *was* chubby then; his mother once showed me a snapshot of a crew-cut, frowning fat boy in husky-sized jeans) lugging the cheap, lurid newsprint while kids from school wheel by on their Schwinns. Taunting, calling him "Preacher Boy." That ten-year-old Kim flushes red, staring at his rubber-tipped Keds as they move across shattered concrete and up the next set of front steps. He's furious at his mother for making him do it and at the same time he wants to protect her white freckled arms and sloping shoulders, her dazzled devout gaze, from their scorn.

On bartending jobs (no one ever questioned a sixteen-year-old handing out liquor), I slid a hand into the back of Kim's waistband, rubbed against him as he poured a scotch for another guest, making Kim flush. I did it because I was newly aware that I could. I'd heard him and Andy groaning with lust behind me when I jumped, in miniskirt and net stockings, from piling to piling in front of the Boston Aquarium. When I answered the door to Quincy F-22 one night, I watched Kim's classmate, dropping by for exam notes, go silly and stuttering, because, as he told Kim later, he never "expected to see a girl *like that* here." I—a former ugly duckling—had become *a girl like that.* Thirty years later I can still remember the snug little midnight blue velour top I wore with a knotted silk scarf, the dusty rose miniskirt. It's as incomprehensible to me now that I could have inspired such silly awe as that Kim could have died as he did.

The boys in the Quincy House dining room, not yet enlightened or intimidated by feminism, tapped their glasses with knives to signal approval when I walked by carrying my tray—while I, trapped in my obsession, fretted over the breading on the cutlets or if the steam table greens were buttered. Despite these attentions, I had to ask Kim twenty times a day, "Do you think I'm pretty? Do you love me?" Kim was a mirror in which I had to constantly check my existence, just as I had to look for myself in every car and shop window. Narcissism is often the price of absence, abuse, and neglect. My biggest fear most of my childhood was that I wasn't real; the flip side was that no one was real to me. At sixteen and still at twenty-six, I was incapable of truly seeing Kim. He was a parent to me, an appendage, a safety net, but never a separate person.

When my nephew was four, I watched him dance before my father, saying "Hi Grandpa! Hi Grandpa! Hi Grandpa!" My father was unable or unwilling to acknowledge his grandson's existence. Growing up, I'd considered my father's rejection normal, just as I accepted that my father, who ate in the dining room while we ate in the kitchen, refused to eat with us because he found our presence too annoying. We knew enough to duck when he told us we were "cruising for a bruising." Because kids have no choice, I took for granted the fact that my father found his children at best repugnant, at worst a target for rage.

My little daughter wraps her arms around her daddy's neck. She draws pictures on Tom's back with magic markers, climbs up his thighs and does flips off his chest. Together they plant daffodil bulbs around our house and fish for bass in the Connecticut River. She kisses and kisses and kisses him and I thank all the powers that I am gratified instead of jealous. At seventeen, when I traveled to Colorado with Kim and heard him call his six-year-old sister "Little One," saw his father lift her onto his lap, I was ashamed of my envy. It was a loss I didn't even know was there, a way of being I hadn't known existed.

Thirty years later I wonder how it is possible to conjure the past, and on what terms. Everything I remember about Kim is distorted by my limitations when I was with him. A twisted Heisenberg Uncertainty Principle, in which the observer subsumes rather than merely affects her subject.

This then is my caveat emptor. I knew Kim better than anyone did; I was incapable of knowing Kim.

At sixteen I noted that Kim wasn't like the rest of the obnoxious Quincy House boys at the dinner table who tried to best each other in pretentious arguments. He didn't need their approval to know his own worth. Nor would he follow any particular party line. Although he disapproved of the Vietnam War, Kim hated the Harvard boys who got fake doctors' letters for their draft boards so they could be designated 4-F. He didn't think it was right for them to let the townies go in their place. *He* wouldn't do it.

"You mean you'd fight in Vietnam?" I asked incredulously. While my own politics were fairly flimsy, they followed along the lines of my classmates and their liberal Democrat parents who drove vw busses with peace signs and taught at Harvard and MIT. The irony of all this didn't escape me, since my father's factory in New Hampshire was busy churning out army boots for Vietnam, boots that bought the clothes I wore, the food I ate.

"I'm not saying that I'd fight necessarily," Kim amended. "I'm just saying everything has a price. You've got to pay some price for what you believe. You shouldn't just get off scot-free."

"Could you be a conscientious objector?"

"No, because I'm not against fighting when it's justified."

This was no abstract college discussion. Kim—whose parents never could have paid his tuition—had come to Harvard on an ROTC physics scholarship, the price of which was four years of service after graduation, which meant, most likely, Vietnam. Deciding whether to give up a scholarship supported by the military, whose actions he'd come to deplore, was a continuing torment.

Though he scorned his mother's religion, Kim was deeply concerned with being a moral man. In one of the few childhood stories he told me, he was seven or so and followed a group of older boys up on a neighbor's roof, from which they threw a kitten to its death. He was appalled that he'd been afraid to try to stop them; he'd wanted too much to belong. Early on he'd decided that to be "one of the gang" was to lose yourself. Acceptance meant a loss of conscience, and Kim was a man of conscience.

He wouldn't let townies die in his place. He wouldn't pretend to be a conscientious objector. He didn't believe in getting off scot-free.

He had to pay for his choices. He didn't need to attend classes. He refused to wear seat belts, to admit to physical fear of any kind. "I'll never die," he assured me, only half-joking. "They'll have a cure for whatever I get by the time I get it." It wasn't long before I couldn't imagine existing without him. The fact of me was predicated on the fact of him. He was elemental, the rocky crust supporting the earth's shifting sands.

Still I was critical, measuring Kim by the perfection I desired for myself. The first time I put my hand around his waist, crossing a street, I was surprised by the softness there. A small, spongy roll hidden by the Oxford shirts. He looked nothing if not straight and tall and lean. His face all angles and planes, highest of cheekbones from a Sioux great-grandmother. Those little love handles came, I imagined, from the two Milky Way bars he bought each afternoon. And he combed his hair oddly, trying to hide the slight recession of his hairline at his temples. Though he generally seemed at ease with himself, one day I idly flipped open the glove box of his car and discovered (on top of the unpaid parking tickets) something called "A Man Stick," a roll-on makeup that explained the orange cast I sometimes noticed on his skin.

"What's this for?" I asked, a small clench in my chest because I'd caught him in a vulnerability.

"I don't like how pale I get in winter," he explained.

I put the stick back but never saw that orange tint again.

One afternoon, I sat in Kim's room doing my homework while he went to deliver a paper for a class. I looked out the window. He was coming through the wrought iron gate, straight and stiff in his green fatigue jacket, his face set as a mask. Something in me lurched; approaching across the icy quad, Kim looked alien. Was this his face when he thought no one was looking, or the face he put on for the world? I turned away so he wouldn't catch me, hurriedly returned to the photocopies of *Collier's Magazine* articles I'd found in the Widener Library using Kim's ID. Please, I thought, don't let me be scared by not loving you. If I didn't love Kim I'd be no one again, plunged back into the abyss of a high school misfit with a bad family.

These moments were few, though, the qualms of any lovers or soon-to-be lovers, I assumed. In our basement rec room, my parents a floor above, Kim and I petted furiously while the turntable spun on the record player. In his dorm room, we could remove our clothes, press flesh.

I loved it, the warmth, the frisson, the excitement, the knowledge that Andy suffered alone on the other side of the wall in his room. I loved Kim's chest, the press of his lips, the cleft of his chin, the jut of his Adam's apple, the bristle of whiskers, his wide, columnar neck. His thighs thick with muscle and curly haired. The way he grew hard, transformed by my touch. The heat, heat, heat of him.

"After you go home," he said, "I sniff my pillow for your scent. I want to hold every bit of you as long as I can." At my parents' house he declared, "If I have a daughter, I want her to grow up just like you did so she'll turn out just like you."

His love-sotted blindness infuriated me. How could he doom a child to my family, my troubled mind? He'd witnessed both by then.

In Kim's suite we sat on the floor in front of the fireplace. Caught in one of my inexplicable periods of paralysis, I huddled with my arms wrapped around my knees. Unexpected as an unscheduled eclipse, darkness had descended. In these moods I couldn't move, could barely speak. It didn't matter that I had a boyfriend who loved me or that my future was full of promise. This darkness had its own volition. I didn't know about depression; I had no name for that which had kept my mother in her room with the shades drawn while we kids ate Sugar Smacks out of little waxed boxes and sent ourselves off to grade school. I was twenty-five years from learning about conditions as biochemical and absolute as diabetes. I did know of my father's happy pills—the Elavil that made him giddy—and how frightening it was when they wore off and he plunged into a meanness worse than before he took them.

Kim poked a log on the fire, leaned back on his arms. He was puzzled by my misery. "Oh, kid. I don't get it," he said, pained. "I just can't stay depressed. If I get down I just drive to the beach and sit there and look at the waves and after a while I have to start laughing at myself in the face of all that enormity. It's a matter of perspective."

His perspective scared me. I found no solace in my own insignificance, as he did. Insignificance equaled nonexistence. I was prone to panics in which I trembled, mute and crouching, saw myself a speck in the cosmos, eons turning somersaults around me. I recognized all time to be a construct, my own life nothing but a blink.

To me, a night sky was terrifying in its limitless scope while Kim looked at the stars and imagined space travel. It was his fervent wish, the boy who'd flown fighter jets in ROTC. The westerner who said that mankind's destiny was to continually explore and take risks.

He couldn't understand my affliction any more than he—who slept so deeply in his sagging dorm cot beside a whistling old steam radiator—could understand how, since childhood, I spent at least one night each week not sleeping at all, thrashing and turning in my bed. And when I did sleep, I suffered nightmares. I was awed by Kim's mental health. It was mysterious and wonderful.

Still, on nights like these I asked him to drive me home before my curfew. I knew that I would be unable to pull myself from this undertow, that I had to hold my breath. We rode quietly through the Cambridge streets, my fingernails cutting my palms.

I didn't know yet that Kim had his own fears and doubts, and when he wrote of them during our first separation, when he returned to Colorado for Christmas break, I couldn't absorb or acknowledge them. I accepted these letters as proof of his love, ignored the awkward slips into a formal, academic voice as he struggled to name his feelings.

> Without a word from or to you in a week—or a short decade—
> I have realized a frightening insecure mind . . . I suppose in a
> way to never be sure about the thoughts and feelings of anoth-
> er person, even in the closest embrace (and perhaps this is why
> I have been so careful with you) let alone at a great distance
> is good. It protects one from assuming too much and from in-
> dulging in unfounded illusions.
>
> Loving you, I need to touch you, probe you, search you with
> a passion to know all of you, everything of you.
>
> I hate lying awake because stillness is so frightening when
> you have so much to remember and so little you can do about
> it. Have you ever tried putting your arms around a dream?
>
> It's painful, Laurie, honestly painful. I love you.

It's chilling now to read those lines. He was foretelling his life fifteen, twenty years down the line. I've imagined him lying awake in fleabag hotels, unwilling to give up on the memory of the Laurie and Kim of that 1970 photo, unwilling to go on. Just as I'd been unwilling to give up on the idea of a Kim who couldn't be frightened by anything, much less stillness.

To understand what happened to Kim and me, why I was so susceptible—and damaging—to him, you have to understand that my childhood was shaped by terror and rage and longing. Why he was so susceptible to me is the harder question.

I lived in fear and I lived in joy. I rode in horse shows. I had a basement workshop. I painted and sculpted and wrote stories and made jewelry and took lessons in dance and copper enameling and drawing. I was teacher's pet that year I met Kim, the beloved favorite of a gentle crippled Boston Brahmin English instructor. I was anorexic, precocious, compulsive. My instinct for life and my instinct for self-destruction were neatly balanced.

I stand on the stairway. My sister, who has just been beaten by my father, sobs and shrieks. My father has climbed in bed to hold her, comfort her while she cries. I, who refuse to cry, am jealous. Although I've been beaten, I've never been held like that.

That child can't be me, any more than the girl Kim fell in love with, that slender sixteen-year-old, unmarked in any way that shows, could have been. Mostly now, I live in peace, on a Vermont hillside with my husband and child, my horses and dogs. My parents, long divorced, join us for Thanksgiving dinner. We all go on as if none of it happened. In fact, my father truly believes none of it did happen. As his memory slips precipitously, he is granted the comfort of more than denial—the world is rewritten as he would have liked it to be. "I never hit you kids," he insists.

There's still no continuity to my internal narrative just as, eventually, there was none to Kim's. No one knows how Kim tied his beginning and end together. Are there people out there who don't doubt they are the same person they always were, who look back at their lives without puzzlement, who see the days, weeks, months, and years, the remembered scenes and conversations, as all steps on a great ladder? Or perhaps a twirl on time's Möbius strip? While I view my history as disconnected fragments, fractured as the lifeline on my palm.

A week after Kim's return from Christmas break, I abruptly decided
we should have "real" sex on my birthday. I didn't want to turn seventeen and still be a virgin. A year ago, only the slutty girls in my high
school were sleeping with their boyfriends, but now sex was hip. The
Age of Aquarius had seeped into Lexington. Vietnam Vets against the
War had camped on our Battle Green, rolling in behind the Minuteman statue with their wheelchairs and rage. Though Kim and I had
both missed Woodstock the summer before we met, while he suffered seasickness on a navy destroyer in the Gulf of Mexico, I had attended the Newport Jazz Festival with a boy I hadn't much liked. He
stuck my hand into his pants while Sly and the Family Stone roused
the crowds. With Kim I was sure it would be different. We were going to Make Love.

We would also, for the first time, get to spend a whole night together. My parents unwittingly obliged by heading north to ski, allowing me to stay home alone for the weekend. My fourteen-year-old brother, Charlie, was back in the Maine prep school from which he'd come home skinny, with circles under his darting eyes, newly versed in acid and coke.

Dinner was in the oven. I ferried two plates, silverware, and glasses to the kitchen table. Our overbred collie, her head shaped like a racing bike seat, scrabbled to get out of my way. She wasn't allowed out of the kitchen because her pedigreed hair might blemish the wall-to-wall carpets, so she lived in fear of being stepped on. I didn't think to set up in the forbidden dining room. I flicked on the tiny tabletop television, flicked off the nightly body count from Vietnam, the usual accompaniment to our burgers, along with my dad's shouts from the dining room that his chops were burned. I checked the clock, pictured Kim maneuvering his way through Friday night traffic. Behind the wheel, all Kim's politeness and easygoing ways evaporated. He cursed and honked with abandon. Woe to the driver who cut him off, or to the elderly woman who forgot to signal. "Old ladies should be drowned at birth!" Kim would shout, roaring up to a rear bumper, gunning his engine, revealing a hint of the rage he kept so carefully hidden.

Then Kim filled the doorway, kicking fresh snow off his battered sneakers. I threw my arms around his neck, breathed in the warmth, and kissed his fresh shaved, cut-spotted chin. "Trying to do yourself in?" I asked.

He fingered a shaving nick. "You'd think I'd know how to shave by now. Mmmm, smells good in here." He held out a small wrapped box. "Happy birthday, Laurie."

"Hey!" I yanked off the ribbon, stripped the paper, and opened the small white cube of cardboard. Inside, on a cushion of cotton, lay a card pinned with two tiny jade ear studs. Hadn't he noticed that I only wore hoops and dangly earrings? Didn't he know me better? I faltered; was our union less than perfect? "They're really pretty," I said, setting them aside.

He glanced regretfully at the gift, registering his failure.

"Are you hungry?" I asked.

"Sure."

I sat primly at the table while Kim buttered his bread, slathered his potatoes with sour cream. I loved to watch other people eat the stuff I wouldn't touch. It confirmed my strength over my body's low-ly desires.

When he led me up the staircase I thought, *I'm going to be changed. I'll never be the same. I'll never be a kid again.* Nostalgic, already, for a state of innocence I hadn't yet lost. Sweetly nostalgic, because I knew there'd be this terrific payoff. I was going to enter this deep mystery that grownups kept for themselves, this amazing pleasure. I was go-ing to love Kim wholly now, with all of me.

We didn't have the nerve to use my parents' king-size bed. Instead we lay down on my narrow twin with the spindly posts, in a room my mother had decorated according to her Colonial phase: hand-paint-ed dressers, walls papered in a tiny monotonous print, olive and rust and mustard, colors I still detest. A room in which I wasn't allowed to hang a poster.

I began my litany of his old girlfriends. "Do you love me more than Marilyn? Than Ginger?"

Kim took my face in his hands. "You don't know the answer to that yet? I've never loved anyone like you. With them I was just biding time. Maybe I didn't know that until I met you, but it's true."

I touched his hair, golden in the light from the hall filtering through my open door. He loved me. And I hadn't eaten anything bad. I was safe. Kim slid my sweater off, my jeans. He unhooked my bra, pulled my bikini bottoms down my jutting hips. He was reduced to a groan then. His jeans on the floor, a condom from the pocket. Kissing, ca-ressing my breasts, sliding down, down, stroking, stroking.

I want to shout, "Wait! This can't work. You don't know what you're up against." I wouldn't know for years, and even then I wouldn't really know, just possess a kaleidoscope of fragments, fleeting patterns: the tan arm and shimmering Hawaiian shirt of the man who led me into the woods when I was six; a habit of leaving my body, floating above it as though I'd become not Laurie but a wisp of Laurie, disembodied, incorporeal. I still have the ability to lose myself in the design of ceil-ing tiles in order to remove myself from any pain—dissociation, the shrinks call it. You, Kim, a twenty-year-old, you thought you could take this on? You had no more idea of me than I had of you—the frightened boy hiding within the tranquil man.

Kim eased my legs apart, hovered above me—and ruined every-thing.

"Oww!" I protested.

"I have to," Kim murmured, pressing, pressing against me, trying to split that thick membrane, gain entrance, remove the last barrier between us. I gritted my teeth. This persistence, this painful intruder couldn't be Kim. My eyes filled at the betrayal. I removed myself and looked down on the two of us, ridiculous figures thrashing on the bed. Finally he collapsed on me, sighed, and touched my face. "It will be better next time, I promise."

In the morning I was seventeen, a woman of the world. (Though innocent enough to think, when I found blood in my panties, that I'd gotten my period at last.) I made omelets and we ate in the sacred dining room while light streamed through the windows, reflecting off new snow.

That afternoon, Kim watched a football game in our basement rec room, shouting at the players, sipping a beer, all the while writing a term paper. "Run, run, run, run!" he screamed, jumping to his feet, papers flying. I tucked my own feet under my hips, tried to focus on my book. How had I found someone so normal?

My parents took Kim along for a family ski weekend to the elegant Lodge at Smuggler's Notch. Kim shared a room with my little brother. He carried my parents' skis, said "Yes, Mrs. Alberts," "Sure thing, Mr. Alberts." My parents loved him.

"I just worry sometimes that they don't know how grateful I am," he confided over the silver tea service in the lodge's parlor.

In my hotel room mirror, I stared at myself naked, wondering if all this sex was making my breasts grow.

"Did you ever think of yourself as physically inferior?" Kim asked. "I mean really inferior?"

Always. As a Jew in New Hampshire, I'd been called Kike on the playground, believed the music teacher discriminated against me when it came time to hand out the sandpaper blocks and the triangle, preferring the rosy blond kids. In Lexington, by seventh grade I crossed the street when I saw oncoming pedestrians so I wouldn't have to be seen, I knew I was so ugly. I told myself I had to be skinny because I had so many other strikes against me.

Kim was the fat boy who had tried to buy friends with candy filched from his grandfather's filling station. In our secret selves, he was still

Preacher Boy and I was still Pinocchio, my nickname until ninth grade, when I returned from February vacation with two black eyes and a new nose.

I drove to Cambridge with my new license, in my mother's big Oldsmobile station wagon, looking for a "Free School"—part of the new, underground Cambridge—where I wanted to take an art class. Map spread out on the steering wheel at a stoplight on Brattle Street, I smashed into the car in front of me. Two business-suited men slowly climbed out of the car I'd hit. Pieces of red plastic lens lay in dirty slush.

"Are you all right?" I asked. "I'm so sorry." I expected the indulgence that men always granted me now. But they maintained grim faces.

"We don't know yet," one of them said.

A whiplash suit was in the process of being concocted. All I'd done was break their taillight. But my mother's station wagon's hood was crumpled. My father's wrath awaited me at home. After the accident report, the wrecker lugged away my mother's car with its damaged radiator, and I ran, panicked, through a maze of Harvard brick.

"Oh, kid," Kim said when he opened the door to F-22 and found me crumpled there. He drew me to him. I couldn't believe there was a man who wouldn't scream at me for my stupidity, as my father would that night. A man who could say, even if it were his car, "It's just an accident." I was trained to expect rage. I wanted to dissolve in the great relief of Kim's kindness.

Eventually I would drive Kim to rage in its other form: the hardened face, the cold set lines of rage deferred. Kim and I already had two companions to our relationship: my depression and his lust. He tried to assuage the former; I provoked the latter. Soon his jealousy would surface, and, without intention, I'd provoke that too. My body would become our battlefield, as it had always been my own.

I wished we could just lie together, cuddling, instead of having to do it all the time. I still loved all the sweet foreplay, which before we became true lovers had seemed random and purposeless, pure pleasure. Now I suspected that Kim *worked* on me, diligent, ever eager for a response. "Do you like this? This? How about this?" In his Christmas letter he'd written that he needed to probe me, know all of me, but I hadn't understood he meant my body too. Sometimes I caught myself blanking him out, wanting to escape. Always he was there, eyes on mine, relentlessly attentive. I felt like a math problem, a composition to be revised.

"I just want you to feel good," he claimed.

I waffled between eagerness, resistance. At times my body responded against my will and shamed me the way eating shamed me; the shuddering tremor meant I was no longer in full control. I wanted and didn't want this. I wanted to be Kim's lover; I wanted to be his child. I called him endless baby names: Kimmy, Wimmy, Boo Boo. I disliked the word *lover,* preferring girlfriend, boyfriend. *Lover* was too explicit, too . . . moist. I suppose that making love with Kim was too much like incest.

On a spring weekend, Kim shared my fourteen-year-old brother Charlie's clammy basement bedroom at my family's summerhouse on Cape Cod. I came downstairs to wake them in the dark, mildewed room. I climbed into Kim's bed with him, nuzzled up. Was Kim embarrassed before my brother or just helpless with instinct, a young man with a girl in his bed? He was still only twenty, as hormonal as Charlie. Even as I did it, I knew I was showing off, saying to my brother, *See. I have this. This is mine.* Or worse—*see what I have and you don't?* Or worse yet—tormenting my brother with my own desirability. The one thing I did know: although I loved Kim, this was not about love.

It's rare to know the precise moment when an addiction first manifests itself. Once a classmate called me, distraught, from a baby-sitting job: she'd just ransacked her employer's refrigerator and cupboards and didn't know why. I immediately recognized the start of a familiar compulsion. In the basement with Kim and my brother, I'd just entered a future of bad behavior, coerced by something as powerful as the need to starve or binge.

Later that morning, Charlie, Kim, and I romped on a foggy beach. Kim brought firecrackers and they lit them on the sand. I didn't much care for loud explosions, but my boyfriend and unhappy little brother laughed and whooped, lighting fuses and running back. Sand burst into the air like shell fire. Behind them, the sea rolled on gray and implacable, to Portugal and Newfoundland.

Outside the Harvard walls cops in riot gear shot off tear gas, wielded billy clubs. The banks and businesses nailed plywood over their smashed plate glass once again. Elevator graffiti urged death to Harvard President Nathan Pusey. I hung out the window of F-22 and heard one boy in the quad yell to another, "Hey, what's going on? Let's go join them!" Students shot bottle rockets out the dorm windows: riot as lark.

I'd been to only one antiwar rally, a peaceful Moratorium against the War on the Boston Commons. My father had forbidden me to go; when I insisted he couldn't stop me, he said, "I hope you get beaten up." I was disappointed to find sunbathers, balloons, boys asking my name. It had seemed more like a rock concert than a protest rally.

In Cambridge, after Nixon bombed Cambodia and four students were killed at Kent State, skulls were cracked, lungs gassed. Protesters roared and surged like a weird wave breaking against the bricks of Harvard Square. The gates of the dorms were locked; university police stood guard. I was trapped at Quincy House, forced to miss my curfew, which had come to seem ridiculous (what might we do after eleven that we weren't already doing?) given the fact that the whole world had stopped making sense. When things quieted down, we climbed, wet handkerchiefs pressed to our noses to protect ourselves from the acrid smoke, over the Quincy House walls, watched by helmeted cops, so that Kim could drive me home. We were sympathetic witnesses, not participants in this history.

Classes and exams were canceled. Grades shifted to pass/fail. And Kim announced his decision. He could no longer allow the navy to pay his tuition. I know that Kim gave up ROTC because of his antiwar feelings, but I suspect that he was as afraid of losing me if he left for four years as I was afraid of losing him. Now there would be no more ROTC weeks in Corpus Christi, no seasickness on a destroyer this summer, no more turning upside down in jets. There would be no automatic four years of military service upon graduation. There would also be no more ROTC scholarship. Kim pleaded his case to the Harvard Financial Aid authorities. They graciously offered enormous loans.

My psychiatrist thought it unwise to let a seventeen-year-old girl travel across the country with her boyfriend for the summer. My mother resisted his advice. When I asked her about it years later, she said, "I thought it would be good for you, being loved." My father said, "I don't care what you do as long as you don't get pregnant, and if you do I don't want to hear about it."

As with my father's indifference, his cruelty, I never questioned my mother's decision. Would I let my own daughter have such daunting freedom ten years from now? Could I stop her? Perhaps my mother was abdicating her own duties, or trying, through Kim, to make up for my father's failings. Perhaps she didn't know better, or she was convinced that I was much older than I was. After all, since I was four, I'd served as her mother, her confidante.

Kim drove us the entire way to Colorado, nearly nonstop except for a few hours of cramped and steamy sleep in the car at the Delaware Water Gap. We carried our ounce of grass in the glove box and bought cigarettes so I could practice inhaling.

"What town does all this belong to?" I gestured at the plains sliding by the car window.

"It's just county land."

I was puzzled, an easterner who knew nothing of state and county territory, who only knew towns bounded by stone walls, villages with their commons or factory cities with their old brick. To Kim, I realized, all this openness was ordinary. I tended to forget his westernness except when he pronounced words differently, saying "rowt" for route or making the word leisure rhyme with pleasure.

The novelty of the plains quickly wore off. I tired of the flat spreads of cultivation, felt seasick from the endless horizon. I spent a lot of the hours dozing with my head in Kim's lap, his hand caressing my hair. The plains lasted right up to Morrissey. The Rockies stood like an unconvincing painted backdrop eleven miles west. We rolled in, grubby and tired, on the second day.

Morrissey stunned me. Before my family moved to Lexington, we'd lived in a New Hampshire mill town for seven years, and I was accustomed to traveling through the "bad" end of town, near my father's factory, where tenement dwellers hung out on stoops and fought in the streets. But in Nashua there was also the "good" end of town, with colonials, Victorians, and stucco Tudors, where the prosperous lived. I'd been allowed to play only with kids from this section.

All of Morrissey seemed to lie on the wrong side of the tracks. We cruised past low bungalows and squat ranch houses painted improbable hues. A toddler in a drooping diaper sat in the dusty road, unattended. Hoods who, according to Kim, fought each other with chains, congregated at a burger drive-in. Morrissey possessed one commercial main street of low, dreary storefronts—a gas station, neon-lit bars, a Mexican restaurant. In all directions beyond town, the fields stretched out, barbed wire enclosed grazing lands, plowed earth, cottonwoods jutting out of the drainages. The brilliance of the light hurt my eyes. The air shimmered. All the moisture had been sucked up in the sunshine.

The Janiks lived in a neat turquoise ranch house. I stood awkwardly as Kim's mother, with a cry of delight, burst out to hug him. Gloria Janik had pale skin, through which green veins ran, forking at her temple, and a sweet birdie face, with a long narrow nose, Kim's high cheekbones, and a small chin. She leaned back to look at him, her face filled with adoration. No matter if he sneered at her Bible; Kim, I saw, adored her too.

Gloria, just home from eight hours as a receptionist at a doctor's office, loaded the dinner table with enough dishes for a buffet. Pickled beets, cucumbers, cottage cheese, Jell-O mold, radishes from the garden vied for space with a baked ham, scalloped potatoes, and a noodle casserole, to be followed by homemade pie. Terrified of so much food, I wondered if I could get away with cottage cheese and cukes.

John Janik, his face kind, square, and freckled, sat bare chested, buttering a radish, at the dinner table. I'd never seen a grown man sit down to dinner with his shirt off. An open-heart surgery scar ran from one collarbone, across his chest like an obscene pink sash, and disappeared around his back. His naked belly jutted against the table.

"Well, well, well, what the h . . . eck!" John intoned, delighted at his joke.

Gloria bustled back and forth to the sink, refrigerator, table, barely sitting down. Kim's younger brother, Matt, who'd just graduated from high school, came in late. He was shorter than Kim, dark haired, light eyed, square faced like his father, overweight and genial. He was seventeen or eighteen and about to get married. Kim often grumbled about Matt. "He does such stupid things! He never thinks. He blew up a tire in his face overinflating it. He makes my parents worry. He's too damn young to be getting married, the idiot."

Six-year-old Sue, freckled and stolid, glowered at me across the table. She wasn't accustomed to sharing her big brother's affection.

Someone knocked on the door. "Oh, no," Kim said, rolling his eyes. "The Avon lady."

"Mom," Matt said, grinning, "you better put out another ham."

"Matthew Paul! Hush!" Gloria opened the door to a breathless, overweight woman with a tight poodle perm.

"Hi Glorie, hi John. I saw a strange car and had to know what was going on!" She glanced about the table eagerly.

"Kim's home with his girlfriend," Gloria explained. "This is Laurie. Will you have some dinner with us, Ellie?"

"Oh I couldn't, well . . . maybe just a little of those scallop 'taters. You make 'em so good, Glorie."

An unfamiliar car worthy of a visit? Where was I, in Mayberry? I shook my head at the provinciality, yet I was awed by the peacefulness of Kim's family, the joviality, the open-arm welcome extended to me, to this nosy neighbor. The only guests my parents had were business associates—leather salesmen, other shoemen—and when my father decided the visits had gone on long enough, he got out the vacuum and rumbled around their legs. He had mocking names for all of them: Laughing Boy, Froggy.

This was America. This was normal. This was the world of TV shows I'd been raised on. Well, John Janik with his bare gut and his scar, his warehouse work, wasn't Darren off to the ad agency or the mysteriously professional Mr. Cleaver, but, taken down a socioeconomic notch, this was it. Okay, there were no books but the Bible and a stack of *Readers' Digests* in the bathroom, but they had produced Kim in all his brilliance and he loved them.

While Gloria did the dishes, shooing away help, John took me for a tour of his backyard. Kim told me that when his parents had bought the house, it consisted of only two small bedrooms, a living room, and a kitchen. But the picture window had looked across the plains to the snowy Rockies and Arapaho glacier. Since then new houses blocked their view. John had added on a boys' bunk room and a family room, and where the picture window had been he hung a large color photo, faded as a pizza parlor travel poster, of the mountains he could no longer see. He also managed to buy an extra lot behind his own, which gave him more room for his elaborate gardening projects.

John was proud of his thriving young black walnut trees and the canna lilies whose bulbs he dug up and hid away each fall in the crawl space under their house. They had their own well, John explained, so he could water his lawn and flowers even when the town banned watering. He'd recently built a little fish pond in the far corner of the lot. Kim said that next year he'd probably move it to another corner. There was always work to be done with a shovel, a wheelbarrow, dirt.

Kim filled me in: John was the son of a Polish coal miner in Wilkes Barre, Pennsylvania, who quit working and pulled John from school when he was in ninth grade, ordering his son to go down into the mines and support him. John escaped, carried to the Southwest to plant trees with the Civilian Conservation Corps, a New Deal program. He was denied a stint in the service during the war because of a childhood bout with rheumatic fever, which damaged his heart; instead he went to D.C. to work on plane engines. There he met a sweet-natured prairie girl, Gloria, with narrow shoulders and a soft, wide bottom. Her family was from Kansas, Scots-Irish, with Indian blood mixed in. John fell for Glorie and gladly put the East behind him when they married and settled in Morrissey. John had worked in his father-in-law's garage along with Gloria's brother until disagreements led John to seek work in the ski boot factory.

Gloria was the brains of the family, Kim told me, but she'd buried them in religion when John went under the knife. She had, he believed, made a pact with Jesus to devote her life to him if he spared John, and she kept her word, rising at five each morning to study her Bible before the house awoke. It was the only source of conflict between his parents, Kim said. His father hated how much time and money she devoted to her church.

That night, I lay in Sue's bed, in her impossibly frilly lavender room, filled with lace and dolls. Kim seemed miles away in the bunk room; I knew it was unlikely that he'd sneak in to visit me. Sue's room shared a wall with his parents' bedroom, and he'd never do anything to hurt them. I'd observed something startling that evening. While Gloria was drying dishes, John had walked up behind her and gave her a big slap on her bottom. She jumped, laughed, and continued wiping and humming her hymns.

In the morning, a flurry of whispers stopped when I walked into the kitchen. After his parents went to work, Kim explained that Matt had gotten his girlfriend pregnant and that's why they were getting married. Last night he'd taken her on a ride at a carnival and she'd thrown up for hours afterward. "Stupid," Kim griped. "Stupid, stupid, stupid. This guy's ready to be a father? Give me a break."

Their next-door neighbor Ana Garcia showed up midmorning, a short, heavy Mexican American woman in her fifties bearing gifts for Kim—homemade tortillas and a jar of her pickled hot peppers, which Kim loved. She always sent him off in the fall with a jar to take back to Harvard. Kim's little sister called Ana "Gramma." The story went that when Gloria wanted to go back to work after Sue was born, John insisted she could do so only if Ana would baby-sit. Morrissey was a town of racial tensions and bigotry, but the Janiks and the Garcias ran in and out of each other's houses like family.

Ana reached up and Kim leaned way, way down so they could hug. "Oh, Kim, it's so good to see you. You know I worry when you're back there. And this is your girlfriend Laurie. Glorie's been telling me about her. She could be Mexican, you know?"

I could have been, according to the pictures of ourselves we took in a Woolworth's photo booth in Boulder that afternoon. I stare into the camera while Kim kisses me. My face is tanned, my black hair winds around us. His light hair flops, and he's adorable. I wear a puck-er-stitched dress with capped sleeves that could be a child's baby-doll nightie. I sit on Kim's lap, one arm around his neck, the other clutching his shirt.

Though John probably would have preferred spending his Saturday in his garden, Kim's parents drove Kim and me and Sue north to Estes Park for a dude ranch barbecue so I could see the "real" West. After supper, Kim and I walked through an alpine meadow, holding hands, eager for time alone. The grass rustled around us, yellow, tall, full of the evening alpenglow.

"Your parents are really nice," I said. I felt embarrassed for them, paying for this touristy show of "western" life when they had so little money. They were stunningly generous to their children, providing the boys with cars. Whatever my father gave was used as a means of control; he constantly threatened to take it back if we even looked at him wrong. But Kim's parents enjoyed giving to their kids. "Can they afford to take us out?" I asked.

"Oh, they can afford this. It's the bigger stuff I worry about. Decisions about their finances, plans for retirement, they can't figure that out for themselves. I have to take care of them."

He meant it. I wonder, now, how long they'd been deferring to Kim's greater knowledge or expecting him to take on this parental role. It's possible, I suppose, to lose your childhood to parents who love you as well as to those who don't. And maybe just as damaging.

Finally, we packed up the Malibu with our canvas tent, heavy flannel sleeping bags, boxes of food, cookstove, and bags of clothes and set out on my first tour of the West. Above Denver we wound through passes with sheer drops and no guardrails. I expected more of the continental divide than dirty lumps of last year's snow clinging to treeless rock. The air was thin and chilled. The mountains spread in all directions, sere brown, geometric points and sweeps of crumbled stone. Were these the mountains in which his father had taken him fishing and a professor from Colorado State had brought him to identify wildflowers when he was in junior high? I'd imagined the Alps, something out of *The Sound of Music*, like up in Estes Park, not this harsh landscape. Abruptly, I saw a chasm between our worlds as ominous and unknowable as these drab, outsized peaks.

It didn't strike me as odd that we should travel for weeks sequestered from other humans. I had no group of friends at school to compare with, no sense of what young people our age did when they traveled, especially in 1970. Andy and his younger brother Leon had traveled the West with Kim and Matt the summer before, and I wanted only to repeat their trip. Mostly, we were contented travelers, holding hands before a campfire, snuggling in our sleeping bags. I wasn't lonely for other company, happy to play Scrabble in our tent on a rainy day, to watch the miles slide by through the windshield as Kim drove, one hand on my breast.

Two incidents occurred, though, one minor, one more significant, that made me wonder. In a campground, a family, packing up their gear, offered us half a package of bacon they didn't want. Kim refused to take it, explaining to me emphatically, "I don't take things from people." I thought it silly, his intensity suspect. It was emblematic of something, but at seventeen, I had no idea what. In the second instance, I spoke to a stranger and paid dearly for it. In Yellowstone we cadged inner tubes from a garage outside the park's borders and spent a wild morning riding rapids in a river with a narrow, flumelike chute. In the afternoon, Kim decided to go fishing. I sat on the riverbank in a bikini, reading. The water burbled, and slanting afternoon light reflected off the rocks and ripples, caught in the wings of insects flitting above. Eventually a squat, longhaired guy wearing a bandanna over his forehead sat down beside me.

"What a righteous day, huh? My name's Cody, you know, like Buffalo Bill? So what are you, Italian or something?"

"Jewish."

"Yeah, far out, I can see that. You got a Jewish body."

Jesus. I glanced at the book in my lap, wishing this idiot would disappear.

"Yeah, I had a Italian girlfriend once. But I got tired of her. I call it the S.O.S. effect. You know, Same Old Snatch."

Kim emerged from a grove of aspens, shirtless, strong legs revealed by cutoffs, a golden vision bearing trout on a forked stick. I scrambled up, pleased to see him, pleased to be rescued. "Hey!" I called.

Kim, jaw stiff, walked right past me.

"That your man? Looks like he's got a problem," Cody declared, retreating hastily.

I was astonished that Kim would feel threatened by this nobody, dismayed that he would trust me so little. Wasn't I allowed to *talk* to anyone? He was jealous before he had reason to be. After an icy hour Kim apologized for being a jerk and cooked the trout for our dinner.

Years later, when things grew ugly between us, he told me, "I knew from the day we met I'd never be able to keep you." The depth and duration of his insecurity shocked me. It had been obscured by his arrogance, that particular Harvard brew. How could a boy who thought his professors had nothing to teach him feel unworthy of an eleventh grade girl? I didn't want to hear it, even then preferring his certainties.

When we hit the West Coast a great uneasiness entered me. I could feel the magnetic pull of the East, a visceral sense that I was not where I ought to be. The bald California hills spread like a rumpled yellow blanket were too foreign. The sun setting instead of rising over the sea made me queasy. At Point Reyes I was overwhelmed by the waves bashing against the coast, the great stacks of rock offshore, the enormous wet redwoods. I dreamed that I was watching the Golden Gate Bridge collapse in an earthquake, a great undulation of steel and asphalt. Searching through the water, I found my mother's drowned face. Homesickness tormented me all the way to Seattle. When I called home my parents yelled at me for phoning collect and both of them seemed mad at me for being so far away. Their anger and misery drew me as strongly as the earth's magnetic pull. I wanted to go home.

Back in Morrissey, Kim drove me to a pay phone outside a liquor store so I could arrange a flight. Colorado sunshine spilled relentlessly onto the sidewalk, the building's faded paint. I squinted against its insistent brightness. A dark-skinned man with shaggy black hair exited the store with a six-pack under one arm.

"You said you'd stay for Matt's wedding," Kim accused, rigid with outrage. "We were going to drive back together."

"I'm sorry, I just can't." I searched his face for the usual empathy but his eyes had turned the cool blue of gas jets. I cracked the car door, stepped out. I needed to get out of here; this was too naked a landscape, it offered no solace. Kim offered no solace—he'd failed to subsume his needs to mine and I no longer recognized him.

As soon as I got home I was slapped into Pratt Diagnostic, the Tufts teaching hospital, for a week of tests to find out why I, nearly a high school senior, still had no periods. I shared a room with a dying woman. Her face was swollen from steroids; her husband and two teenage daughters came in every day to vent their anger at her for not being home. I had no visitors. My father forbade my mother or brother to come, since it was his vacation week at the Cape and he didn't want it disrupted.

For a week I was prodded and poked by my doctors and a gaggle of male medical students, who pulled up my Johnny gown to analyze my level of development as well as to remark on my tan. "My God, you're black!" my endocrinologist, who had earlier accused me of wanting to look like a concentration camp victim, cried as he and his entourage gaped at my nakedness. Med students were assigned to sit beside my bed and ask questions such as "Do you prefer cuddling to intercourse?"

Kim sent jokey, apologetic cards. In one reference to the scene at the pay phone by the liquor store, he admitted to playing the martyr and enjoying self-pity. He bemoaned the minuscule chance of Congress passing a Volunteer Army and the fact that he hadn't taken biology courses since med students could avoid the draft. He kidded that he was practicing his marching. "Now don't get upset," he wrote.

The doctors put me into insulin shock to calibrate my hormone levels, measured my wrists to see if my bones had fully ossified (they hadn't), and concluded, "The real problem is that she doesn't want to be a woman." No one spoke of anorexia then, much less understood it, just as no one had objected earlier when I refused to answer an emergency room intern about the source of my swollen, battered eye. "Who did this to you?" the intern had asked, but didn't pursue it.

Did I want to be a woman? I didn't want to be like my subjugated mother, and I saw her weight problem as evidence of her weakness. I wanted control; I wanted power and the only control and power I'd managed was over my body and its desires. I mistakenly believed that power over my body was the one thing my father couldn't steal from me.

At the hospital I wandered in my bathrobe, sulking, incarcerated but not sick. One day, a beautiful young black man hailed me in the patients' lounge. "How are you on this fine day?" he said.

"I'm bored," I told him. "And lonely." I was surprised by that admission, embarrassed that under my bathrobe I wore a Johnny gown.

"Would you like some company?" His name was Calvin; he worked downstairs in the kitchen and was visiting his sister, a nurse on the ward. He wanted to go to school to be a lab technician. He had curly lashes, smooth dark skin, and a gentle voice. His big knees angled the loose scrubs he wore. When he asked me out I declined, saying I had a boyfriend. But it was only partially out of loyalty to Kim. I was afraid of Roxbury, where Calvin lived, and I still thought of myself as a girl who dated Harvard boys. When Kim returned, I didn't tell him about Calvin, but I didn't forget Calvin's exquisite face or the pleasure of his wanting me. If this were the power granted women, I'd take some.

Winter 1997

Here in our house in Vermont, Tom ran a wire from a pine tree to our living room window, hung bird feeders. Squirrels were the first to find them. We had to slide the feeders farther along the wire so the squirrels couldn't jump from the tree. One just tried and fell, but then he leaped from the snowy ground and made it, scrabbling onto the tipping feeder. We'll have to hang it higher. I don't really begrudge the squirrels. I enjoy their antics, their twitching tails and the way they traverse the wire suspended upside down, paw over paw, like a kid on a ropes course.

What does this have to do with Kim? Now I am the one taking solace from nature, as Kim once said he did. I with my body chemistry corrected. My husband and child asleep upstairs. Snow, crusted, a crisp hard blanket stretches from tree to tree. That is what the medicine is like, it covers. But I know what's underneath. I know because I've stopped taking the pills and the darkness returns immediately, a presence that travels with me, a haunting that flutters about me like bat wings.

What of Kim's medication? When did that start, and why did it cost so much?

My daughter, not yet four, told me yesterday as she was struggling into her snowsuit that the first kid in her preschool class to get into his or her snow clothes gets to be line leader. *Line leader.* Her world, in which it's thrilling, an honor, to be the first to lead the other three-year-olds out to the play yard. I don't remember that emotion but I recognize in its existence the loss of something, a perspective, a view of the world in which small things matter so greatly. It makes me want to go upstairs and climb in bed beside her and nuzzle my nose up to her little hand or against her small smooth back, to touch her sweetness. My great good fortune. Kim, why did you deny yourself this?

Sunday movies, laundry, a nap with Becky while Tom and our neighbor snowshoe, then before it gets dark Becky and I dress for the cold and go out for a walk. She slides down snow banks and the dogs cavort. I have to half-pull her up our long, steep driveway. Inside, she puts on a red summer dress with a big white collar, then retreats to the world of her troll house while Tom and our neighbor warm themselves with bourbon. I make myself a rum drink.

See, Kim, how companionably we drink here, each having just one, maybe two? The woodstove warms us; a child plays nearby, speaking in low, muted voices to her toys. The dogs groan and shift on their mats in the kitchen. This is winter, this is our life.

What am I trying to say to you? I have this and you don't, didn't, never chose to? Lost the ability to? You said you didn't want kids and I didn't believe you. You loved them. Or is it the drink, that we can do this, have one, set it aside, go on with the evening, and you had to keep returning to that bottle? That bourbon bottle I saw in your freezer when you had apartments, in a cupboard in a motel room near Forty-second Street in New York? Your brother says it went past that, came to gallons of cheap vodka and Gatorade, your special cocktail.

I'm angry, contemptuous. You could have had all this and more. You had parents who loved each other, loved you. Who lived in great normalcy, who offered only simple expectations. So why, then?

It's easy to see myself as the snake in this picture. What grandiosity, a friend says. To think I had that power to ruin a life. It's a disease. Even the AMA admits it. Alcoholism, for all its devastations, is so ordinary, so prosaic. Yet what can be compared with it, a disease that changes the personality, removes one from life long before death? But it wasn't just the booze. Kim's disintegration began prior to his drinking getting out of hand. Disintegration is a good word for it. He stopped being integrated.

On my way home from work—I am teaching at a college in Massachusetts, driving down from Vermont—I took a back road off the highway and pulled into the parking lot of one of Kim's regular haunts, the Stanley Motor Lodge, now the Valley View Motel. I had heard from my mother and Matt that Kim stayed there when his employer, a packager of study skills courses for colleges and prep schools, moved its northern office to Massachusetts. I sat in the lot feeling nauseated, shaky. Interstate 91 roared behind the building. No valley view here. For weeks I had stared at the fading paint on that building as I commuted past on the highway, trying to get the courage to stop in. From the outside, it didn't look that bad. Fresh light brown paint covered the motel exterior, though a Bud Lite ad displayed next to the vacancy sign didn't bode well. I entered the dark office. Paper peeling from the walls. A large beer and juice cooler with sliding doors by the entry. A short fiftyish Indian or Pakistani woman came to greet me. I launched in: "Did this used to be the Stanley Motor Lodge?"

"Yes."

"Did you own it then?" Her dark eyes questioning now. Did I sound like some tax investigator?

"I'm an old friend of a man who used to stay here. Kim Janik?"

"Oh, yes." She nodded. "A very nice man. He was my regular. Every year in the winter he stayed."

"He died two years ago," I said.

"What happened? He was a very nice man. A very nice man. The last few years he didn't talk to anyone."

"It was the drinking," I said.

"Yes, yes. The drinking. When I cleaned his room, I found half-gallon vodka bottles. One night, you know, he kicked the walls." She smiled at me, trying to figure out what it is I wanted from her, what I was doing there.

I couldn't—didn't want to—conceive of this Kim, kicking walls, causing damage. "Did he apologize the next day? When he kicked the wall?"

She looked at me uncomprehendingly.

I told her that I hadn't seen him in five years when he died. I lied, it was ten, but I was afraid that ten would make it seem like I didn't have the right to ask about him.

"You were his friend," she said. "Why didn't you help him?"

I gazed about uneasily. "I couldn't be with him. He was in love with me."

"Ah, so that is why. Because you broke off."

"No, no, he drank for a long time before that. I couldn't stand his drinking." An easier truth, a convenient one.

"You are married?"

"Yes."

"You have children?"

"One little girl."

"Ah, of course, you couldn't break your marriage." She nodded knowingly, relieving me from blame. "But he had no one."

"That was one of the things I couldn't stand. He was so isolated."

"Yes, yes. A woman, she must have the social, you know, but not the man. Not the man."

"Oh, my husband is very social. Some men. . . . But Kim, when he kicked the wall, did he . . ." This was important to me—a contrite Kim, apologetic, was preferable, less changed.

She waved me silent. Two grungy women had come in, girls. Prostitutes or junkies, maybe. One wore gray leggings under a waist-length black leather jacket, multiple earrings, heavy makeup. The other was messy, blond, rumpled in flannel.

"Are you staying tonight?" the owner asked these women.

"We don't know. We won't know until we hear from someone."

"Don't you like your room?"

"No." I tried to imagine what this room could be like, that girls such as these didn't like it.

"We can change it. You can be in the other building. There is room now. I will make a call." She lifted the phone.

"We changed our room last night."

"Checkout is eleven," she said. She looked worried.

Finally, the girls negotiated to pay an extra seven dollars to stay in the room until 12:30. It was now close to 11:00. They were waiting for someone to bring them drugs, probably. Is this what Kim lived among? If they turned tricks, did he frequent such women? Or was he beyond that, beyond the lust that plagued him with me?

The girls bought juice and left.

"So," I started again, "did he pay for damages, when he kicked the wall?" Was he still that responsible, did he know what he'd done?

"No damages." She shrugged. "It was his mother's fault. I met her; she came out with his younger brother from Colorado to get him. She was a realtor, you know."

"Yes, a very nice woman," I echoed her wording about Kim. "Very religious. Jesus was everything to her. She thought Jesus would take care of Kim."

"It was her fault," the proprietor insisted. "A mother must find a wife for her son, he must settle down, he must have responsibilities or he has nothing to live for. I have a son, twenty-three. He must marry, have a family, pay bills, you know? So that he doesn't just drift. You must have family. Kim Janik had nothing."

"Nothing to live for," I echoed.

"Family," she said. "You have a husband, a child. These are the boundaries." She put her flattened, upright hand on the counter like a fence. "You know? Women, we live with these boundaries. You, you have a child, a husband, now you must think of them. You must forget the past, forget about Kim Janik, think only of your child or you will make yourself sick."

"Yes," I said, "yes," to please her, to have her think well of me, but of course I couldn't forget. I reached across the counter to grasp her hand. She gripped mine and met my eyes.

"Thank you," I said.

I was sick already. I had made myself sick with Kim's death. He would be aware of the irony of me being drawn to him now. And he, the most private of men, would hate this. So why, then? I need to know what happened, and what part is mine. What would have happened if he'd never met me? Did I come into his life and bend it out of shape, or would he have broken anyway? Was there some fault line running through him? A fault is a weakness, an error, culpability, but also a fracture in the earth's crust accompanied by a displacement of one side with respect to the other. Perhaps it was our fault line, not his alone, and I got to rise as he fell.

"You aren't talking to us," Tom complained that night. I shook myself. "I'm sorry. I didn't realize . . ." I told him about the motel, the woman, and my lie. "I'm going down some long tunnel of sadness," I said.

"As long as you don't get obsessed," Tom said.

That night I woke several times thinking of Kim. What does this mean for Tom, for Becky, I wonder. In the midst of it, I'm only half with them. But am I ever more than half? I love them, and I want to hide. I want to read, to be left alone, alone, alone. I want to lie in a dark room and drift into that half sleep in which the past runs behind my eyes like a movie.

We had dinner at my mother's. She was afraid, she said, that Tom might be jealous of all this attention to Kim's memory. Or maybe it would bother him because of his father's drinking.

"No," Tom said, "that doesn't bother me, but you said you're traveling down some long tunnel of sadness, and if it takes you away from Becky and me I won't like it."

"See," my mother said. When Tom took Becky home to bed, I stayed to help clean up. She brought it up again before I headed home. "Don't talk about it in front of him," she counseled.

As though I could help it. *Who made you the marriage expert?* I wondered. Time had, the way time made Nixon an elder statesman.

"Why do you think he kicked the wall?" I asked Tom that night in bed. It haunted me, the image of Kim alone in that terrible room.

Tom said, "Rage at the world he thought had put him there. At himself."

I try to imagine Kim like the mumbling, raging, incoherent drunks I've known in Alaska, seen in New York. I can't picture him like that. I suppose it's possible that under their spittle, their gin blossoms, their ranting slurred speech, some of them were once as sweet, as clean and hopeful and smooth skinned as Kim used to be.

The fall after our cross-country trip, Kim resolved to become a writer and switched his major to English. I still thought I wanted to be a
child psychologist; at least that's what I wrote on my college applications. I didn't apply to Harvard; it was too close to home.

Kim had so thoroughly replaced my parents, it seemed natural that
he would drive me to my college visits. I'd already been interviewed
for Yale in Lexington by a pale, madras-wearing alumnus with a weak
handshake. At Wesleyan, the interviewer was an overweight young
black man. He asked me, with a knowing smile, "How come all you Jewish girls want to be psychologists?" I was discomfited by his willingness to lump me by ethnicity; I hadn't known I was a cliché

We left Kim's car in New Haven and rode the train into New York.
At the Museum of Natural History, behind diorama glass, painted

steppes rolled away in diminishing perspectives while prehistoric wom-
en pounded skins. A wave of sound rushed through the halls, a roar
like the ocean. Then hundreds of schoolchildren swarmed us, their
voices bouncing off the high ceilings and walls. I imagined the yellow
busses idling outside, the joy of being released from gray classrooms,
the teachers' panic as they counted heads in the shifting, shrieking
hordes. We retreated upstairs to the African exhibit. A cast metal bust
of a woman headed the staircase. Kim and I burst out laughing: the
tips of her bronze breasts had been polished shiny by the hands of
thousands of little kids on field trips.

Outside, leaves skittered and crunched at our feet as we made our
way across the park to the Metropolitan. I took Kim's hand. Without
him, I would have been frightened to walk through New York City. With
Kim, I felt grown-up, urbane, blessed in the golden autumn light.

Such harmony didn't last long. By January, my college applications
were mailed and I had enough credits to graduate high school. I'd been
programmed to seek college entrance since infancy. Without the goad
of academic requirements or friends in classes to draw me, I suddenly
had no reason to go to school. I sank into a grumpy restlessness.

In the new age of "relevancy," I trumped up an independent study
with Mr. Tyler, a hip young teacher who played poker with students,
drove a red Mustang, and held court at the Pewter Pot coffee shop.
Mr. Tyler was in his early thirties, handsome—a sandy-haired ringer
for Marcello Mastroianni, with his square face and blunt nose, a former basketball star in Lexington High School. He took me alone to
Friendly's, where other lunching teachers gave us the evil eye. With
Mr. Tyler's blessing, I wandered Cambridge and Boston, jotting notes
about the Free Schools and macramé shops that had sprouted like
mushrooms in the moist compost of the late sixties:

> I park across the street and glance apprehensively at the slea-
> zy little storefront claiming "Free Dinner Saturdays, bring what
> you can" in a bright sloppy green paint. I peer in the window.
> In the corner on a cot, a boy and girl are wrapped together.
> They seem to be asleep. I knock and watch the couple untan-
> gle. He opens the door. I ask about the Free School. He says
> spacily that someone who knows should be back soon but I
> can read the bulletin board. I know him vaguely. Didn't he go
> to Lexington High School a million drugged light years before?

I don't ask. He sits back on the cot with the girl who wears a green fishnet sweater. Embarrassed, I read the board and decide to forget it. I am frightened by the familiar yet unknown face. They watch me silently. I leave and again they slowly sink back into oblivion.

"Earth Guild"—a little store on a Cambridge side street. Filled with craft books, back-to-nature literature, yarns, macramé strings, looms, metals, candle waxes, molds, various hip craft materials and various hip craft people. Hip lady dances, flirts with bearded man, ignores her child. Nagging, whining child pleads for attention from mother, bearded man, customers.
 "Play in traffic, kid," someone suggests.
 "Take me," cries the child to a leaving hip person.
 "Take me," purrs his mother to the bearded man.
 Not cool.

I wasn't cool either, nor was Kim. Some great shift was occurring around us, and despite our politics, our dope, Kim and I were out of the loop. Sure, a lot of it was sordid, or dumb and tedious like the Hare Krishnas banging their tambourines on Brattle Street. But I was beginning to sense a world beyond classes and libraries, the endless grub for grades. I was also beginning to entertain disloyal thoughts about Kim, who seemed content to write his poems and papers, read his books, while the world went through paroxysms around us.

One morning my father came into my room and sat on my bed. He said, "Your mother wants me to leave." I saw he was crying. Crying? In my room while I was getting ready to go to school? "Nothing makes sense anymore," my father sniffled. "I tried to do right by you kids. I tried to provide, but the world's falling apart. Burning, looting, draft cards. . . . I don't understand anything anymore." He looked pitiful, ugly. I turned away from the sight of him diminished.

Everything was sliding out of control. I was out of control. I'd gained forty pounds since the past August when I'd been put in the hospital for a week of tests. (Granted, I probably needed the first fifteen or twenty.) Before the hospital I'd starved much more than I binged, but for reasons I couldn't decipher, the balance had shifted. Now I didn't recognize myself. My very dimensions had mysteriously altered; I bumped into chairs and tables. I didn't know where I began and ended anymore. I, the girl who had planned her wardrobe two weeks in advance, shuffled around in overalls and work shirts.

I'd like to think that getting fat was an act of rebellion, that I'd taken the attitude, after the hospital: *All right, goddammit, you want me to eat, I'll eat.* But that wouldn't be accurate. For all my supposed independence, my college boyfriend, I was completely unprepared to move into the world on my own. The California coast had revealed my need for my parents, despite who they were; my burgeoning size bespoke my terror at leaving home.

My little girl has owned several kittens taken from their mothers too early; even as adults one sucked its tail and another kept attaching itself to my daughter's neck to nurse. Like me, they couldn't grow out of the hunger for what they'd missed.

Kim, with his uncommon loyalty, insisted I was still beautiful. I clung to his approval and, filled with self-disgust, despised him for it. At night I kicked my sweaty sheets and cursed myself for being such a failure. I'd be going to my third-choice college, a school I'd applied to only because my cousin worked in the admissions office. Despite my good SAT scores, despite winning a state English contest that prompted hundreds of schools to ask me to apply, when they got my applications they'd recognized me for what I was, a lonely misfit. "You should have applied to UMASS," my father railed, ridiculously since the school I'd gotten into was better than UMASS. "You thought you were such a *bigshot!*"

A hot day in early May. I sat with a group of twelfth-grade classmates on the Lexington Battle Green, an impromptu gathering to which I'd tentatively attached myself. Although we'd shared classrooms, I hadn't talked to any of them since eighth grade, when I'd withdrawn and started starving. Rachel, who moved over to make room for me in the circle, smiled shyly. She was a brilliant, ungainly girl with kinky dark hair and skin problems, my best friend until I'd cut her off when my mother accused us of being lesbians.

Fifth, sixth, seventh grade. I'd run fast in the fifty-yard dash and fought with boys who had to see if they could beat up *the girl*. I got detention for talking to my friends in French class. I rode my horse, skated, and tobogganed. In Hebrew School, Pincus Klein wrote petitions to bring back Star Trek and told me, through his spitty teeth, that he had a crush on me. Our teacher announced that Jesus had been fathered by a wandering Roman soldier; the next week, in thrilling Christian justice, she died in a car accident.

I grew nine inches between fifth and seventh grades and, still unself-conscious, wandered the lunchroom begging everyone's desserts because I was starving. When my best friend Rachel came to my house for a sleepover we discovered we had a crush on the same boy. We held hands in bed and I felt the love flow between us like electricity between the poles of Donny Wiener's science fair project.

"Hey, there goes your blond god," David Blauman sneered. Blobby, we'd called him in sixth grade.

I glanced up to see Kim, shirtless in the early heat, riding by on his racing bike, which he kept in my parents' garage. He circled the Battle Green, disappeared behind the Minuteman statue, flashed off. I'd told him I wanted to spend a little time alone downtown. Was he checking up on me? *Couldn't he give me this, just this?* I thought with annoyance and a whisper of guilt.

"The ten-speed Apollo," Emile added.

He was the boy on whom Rachel and I had shared a crush. Why did he and Blobby sound so sarcastic? I didn't know they were aware of Kim, or even aware that I still existed. I guess my having a college boyfriend was an unforgivable affront. But I didn't want a college boyfriend anymore; I wanted to be one of *them.* We were about to graduate and I had missed my entire high school life. I wanted to go back to junior high and do it all over. This time I'd be loyal to Rachel and scream at my mother, *We aren't lesbians, we're friends!* I wouldn't go on that first unnecessary diet that set me spinning into anorexia. I wouldn't have to add up my calories a hundred times a day, wouldn't have to feel tainted if I accidentally took a sip of coffee sweetened with sugar instead of saccharine, wouldn't have to sit in class and listen to the hamster wheel of my obsession spinning: my weight, my weight, my weight. I'd have gone to parties, kissed boys with braces, learned to dance. I'd be normal.

Emile's curly auburn hair caught the afternoon sun. I'd forgotten his shrewd green eyes, his soccer player's physique. Before I'd withdrawn from my classmates in eighth grade I'd written love poems about Emile and hung around in front of his house hoping for a glimpse of his mysterious twelve-year-old life. He'd given me a valentine on which he'd written, "Don't open until I'm away." Inside were sketched two curvy lines indicating a woman's torso and the penciled line: "I thought the heart shape was getting old." Now Emile would be going to Harvard in September. So would Rachel.

As though I were still in junior high, I began to haunt Emile's neighborhood, knock on his door. I pursued him doggedly, shamelessly. I showed up at his house to his parents' bewilderment. I invited him to take walks. He confessed that he'd beaten up a boy in eighth grade who reported sitting in my backyard in the dark, watching me practice dancing with my reflection in the den window. I winced at the humiliation even as I was warmed by Emile's defense of my eighth grade honor.

In the den of my parents' house, the same den in which four years earlier I'd innocently danced with my reflection, and not long ago sat in Kim's lap, I told Kim we needed to talk. Kim, in a pale blue shirt with the sleeves rolled, leaned forward to listen with his usual eagerness. Behind him, a framed charcoal of a peasant mother and child tilted on its hook.

"We haven't been getting along that well lately," I started.

"It's no big deal, Laurie," Kim said. "You've had some disappointments. That's all. You'll get over it."

"No. It's not just that. I'm too young to commit to one person. I need to go out with other boys."

Kim stiffened, paled. I forged ahead, as brutal and self-involved as any teenager trying to escape a loving parent. "I've been kind of getting to know this guy from school, Emile. We were in junior high together, his mother was my French teacher in fifth grade . . ."

"You're breaking up with me," Kim said in a deadened voice.

"We can still be friends," I offered, echoing a million "Dear John" letters. Kim stared at me, rose and strode out of the room. The screen door slapped and then his car engine revved as he backed out of our driveway. Kim had receded from my mind already. All I could see was what I wanted, what I thought would save me, and now it wasn't Kim but Emile. They were just branches to grab onto as I fell.

Was I a branch that Kim was grabbing onto as well? Perhaps. What followed in later years would make you think so, but it's possible that at this stage, at least, Kim was following the normal course of a rejected lover. Though I refused to imagine what he felt as he drove away, or in the weeks that followed, I picture him now moving through his last days of college, weighted by the loss of a girl he believed to be his soul mate, the only one worthy of the gift of his inner life. He eats in the Quincy House dining hall, and the raucousness of the boys around him is an insubstantial buzzing. He completes a final paper on the poems of Coleridge, composes poems and letters with which to inundate me. They come in sheaves, loving, angry, forgiving in turn as he wrestles his loss.

Kim wrote:

> May 27, 1971
>
> . . . I realize that our old love is past, but what I retain is a different sort of love; a compassion, a tenderness, and a concern which do not require you to make any choices, which simply say "I am here, come if you need me." Whatever happens to you in the future, Laurie, and whatever happens to me, nothing will destroy this feeling . . .

It was a promise he kept and kept. In my journal that day I wrote: "Kim sent another letter, more poems. I don't care." How was it that I'd lain beside Kim in a college dorm room and thought of the light that filtered through his discolored window shade as a golden illumination of our love? That particular yellow light had evoked our attachment the way a sepia photograph conveys nostalgia. And now that attachment could be retracted as easily as a window shade.

I chain-smoked and experienced for the first time that female activity: waiting for the phone to ring. My life as a born-again high school student didn't last long. Emile ditched out quickly, put off by my intensity and desperation. In any case, I'd found his friends and their parties boring. Too many bottles of peppermint schnapps treated like the holy Grail, the stupid thrill of breaking into a swimming pool in someone's backyard. As it turned out, I hadn't been missing that much. And though I'd wanted Emile, emblem of the life from which I'd exiled myself, in my arms he'd felt slight after Kim's substantial bulk.

I stopped by unexpectedly at Kim's dorm. The worn stone steps of Quincy House were as familiar as the avocado carpeting that climbed the staircase at home. This *was* my home, my real life. Why had I been so eager to give it up? Kim opened the door to my knock. Are there ways to say it that aren't trite? Yes, his face lit up. As though the rigid straightness of his back, his ramrod self could fall away at the sight of me. I was as relieved as he was. I'd made a stupid mistake.

Kim's parents drove out with Sue, plump and impassive, for his graduation. I was plump and gloomy. To his parents' dismay, Kim collected his degree wearing jeans torn at the knee and a T-shirt. I was disappointed that he'd received his B.A. only *cum laude* instead of *magna* or *summa cum laude*. My version of Kim required him to be the most accomplished, even if I'd failed. Unconcerned, he said he'd changed his major too many times to have enough courses for those honors.

After his graduation, Kim moved into a tiny, roach-infested apartment on Park Street in Boston and started working days at the Lincoln-Mercury garage where he'd been serving as night watchman after he'd given up his scholarship. I couldn't believe this was the life he'd chosen. He had huge loans to pay, Kim reminded me. He was still facing uncertainty about the draft lottery; he'd been issued a fairly high number but no one knew how many men they'd call up. Anyway, what he really wanted was to be a writer, so it didn't matter what job he took or where he lived.

I disagreed. At least Andy (safe from the draft due to a wrestling injury) had an internship at the Woods Hole Oceanographic Institute and spent his time scuba diving and going out on research boats. Kim worked for a car salesman, not such a big leap from his grandfather's garage. I was afraid he'd taken the path of least resistance—he'd had the job so he kept it. It wasn't that he'd been doing anything different in college—reading and writing and working menial jobs. But he'd been at *Harvard*. At *Harvard*, Kim had a cachet, an identity that automatically won the world's approval and so, by osmosis, did I. He didn't seem to mind giving it up, but I minded. Harvard was gone and along with it my specialness. I was just a girl who didn't get into a college she liked. While Kim was happily reading and writing, learning guitar, and playing pickup basketball on the city courts with a bunch of black guys in what he called the "outclassed league," I flailed.

On the last day of high school, as I was walking the two miles home, carrying the end-of-year gleanings from my locker, my high school mentor Mr. Tyler veered to the curb in his red Mustang. He offered a ride. My knees poked up next to the gear shift; the car felt absurdly low. I sweated in the baggy blue work shirt I'd taken to wearing to hide my new body. Tyler let the car idle in our driveway. He turned to me, hands still spread on the steering wheel. "I'm going to miss you," he said. When he reached over I thought he was opening the door for me but he put a hand behind my neck, pulled me close across the jutting gearshift, and startled me with a hard kiss. When he released me I opened the door as though nothing had happened, gathered my purse, my books.

"I want to see you," he said, reaching for my arm. "Can I call? Can I come visit?"

"Okay," I said in what must have been a duck's quack and scuttled away. Once I was over the shock—and the fear that my mother had seen us through the driveway hedge—the possibilities bloomed. I waited for Tyler to call me.

I drove past my own graduation in my mother's car—a sea of blue robes behind chain link, as distant and alien as strangers at a concert. They whooped and threw their mortarboards into the sky, tiny flecks on a playing field.

I sweltered at home, sharing the house with my father while my mother and brother moved to our summerhouse. I had nothing to do all day until Kim showed up after work. My father and I were enemy housemates. He bitched at me for throwing away his moldy cottage cheese and green salamis. "Money doesn't grow on trees," my father lectured. "People have to work for a living, not that *you* care." He was newly angry with me for not having a summer job like my industrious brother and sister who were working at the Cape Cod Mall.

Glancing back, I want to tell that lumpy, sullen Laurie to get a job, quit sulking around the house. It's hard to acknowledge such melancholy indolence without echoing my father. As a girl, I feared being like my mother. As an adult I see how much of my father is in me. When I was twenty-five I joined an eating disorder group. One assignment involved consuming a meal in front of a mirror. I poured out a bowl of cereal, started chewing, and was appalled to see, reflected back at me, my father's hard-jawed, angry face.

One theory about bullies says that they are provoked by the weakness in others that threatens what they perceive as weakness in themselves. I think of my father, younger than his own brother by twenty years, the butt of sadistic family jokes. It provides an explanation for his animosity toward his children, but it was true for me as well. I bullied my younger brother when we were little just as my older sister bullied me, and I bullied Kim because he allowed it. I feared hurting a child.

I never liked babies. I was repelled by their helplessness, their weak necks and feeble spewings. My brother, the father of two sons, says that sometimes when he's angry at one of his boys he feels the tension in his arm as it rises up to strike; it is all he can do to stop the motion. He considers it the success of his life that he hasn't perpetuated that tradition.

I didn't have a child until I was forty. By then I didn't fear physically hurting a child, but I worried that I'd be unable to love it, turn away from it and ruin its life. I was ill with terror my entire pregnancy. I couldn't eat, couldn't gain weight. But when they placed my daughter in my arms I was filled with such simple passion that something was lifted. When she cried in the night and my voice was gentle, the knowledge that I loved and loved wholly made me whole. Then the new terror surfaced: I dreamed of my mother stealing her, hiding her. I lived in dread of abductions, of the silent theft caused by lead paint, the ravages of sexual predators. As Kim long knew, the price of such unchecked love was unbearable loss.

"It's kind of interesting," I enthused about Mr. Tyler to Kim while we were making love. Or rather Kim was making love. Half the time now, when Kim and I had sex, my mind wandered. What he felt about my indifference he didn't say. "Someone so much older," I continued. "You know, just an experience. It's not like it's love or anything. It doesn't have to change things with us." I can see now that sickly complicit half smile as Kim, suspended above me, listened. To be fair, this was 1971, and monogamy was suspect. Open relationships were touted. Besides, if the fling with Emile had shown Kim that I'd disappear to follow my whims, it had also shown him that I'd be back, most likely. Still, I could see him swallow something in that moment—a jagged piece of himself.

It wasn't even a real affair, just a lot of making out in my parents' bed while Tyler waffled over whether or not to betray his pregnant second wife. I didn't really want him—he was too straight, a guy who wore Bermuda shorts and liked to golf. But he was my teacher, married, older and therefore exotic. His visits gave shape to my empty days. When Tyler took the noble course—"I've already messed up one marriage, I don't want to blow it again,"—I plunged deeper into darkness. I started hitching. I walked down our driveway to Massachusetts Avenue and stuck out my thumb, soliciting rides to Cambridge, Boston, just to see what would happen. I signed up for an Outward Bound course, hoping it would shake me from my funk.

In the letters Kim sent me at the Colorado Outward Bound School that August, he was generous with his thoughts, still confident of a willing listener, playful. More than that, he was open to experience, to strangers—he described hanging out on river rocks like an otter in the White Mountains, where he fell in with a bunch of travelers who shared their dope and potato chips—an image of Kim hard to reconcile with who he later became. He was working a dumb job, but deep in the process of trying to find a writing voice. The poems kept coming.

I've always thought that Kim didn't try harder to publish because he couldn't bear the rejection that comes with the territory. It's ironic, then, that he pursued me despite the rejections. But how could he know them as rejections? I wrote him that summer, "We shouldn't have to ever separate totally, should we?"

Surely my Outward Bound patrol didn't share the romantic vision of me expressed in Kim's poems. I was the worst, absolutely the worst, member of a group that contained a proudly virginal Texas Aggie and an Illinois farm boy who did one-handed pushups every morning. Although I'd always been athletic, having just gained forty pounds, I was the slowest, weakest hiker. I could barely lift my pack the first day. I suffered altitude sickness and terror of heights. One instructor threatened to throw my pack over the edge if I didn't step off a cutaway ledge and rappel into a quarry. Once again I couldn't recognize myself: I was the patrol loser.

On a culminating hike without instructors, another suburban Boston girl and I figured out from our topographic maps that we were not far from Aspen. We ditched our earnest patrol and ran away. After three weeks in the wilds the riotous color of a grocery store left us dazed as though tripping. The first man we met, a bland balding guy, offered us a place to sleep and cooked us eggs for breakfast. This was the real adventure, not the fourteen-thousand-foot mountains or being browbeaten into stepping backward off a cliff. This was news: I could go anywhere and the fact that I was young and female meant someone would take me in.

While we were hitching back to face the music at Outward Bound, our ride stopped at the Redstone Hot Springs. We joined naked hippies for a soak. In the bright Colorado light as I sank into the steamy water, I was surprised to see that I had lost a lot of the weight I'd gained; I'd trudged it away over mountains, and my legs were sinewy from the forced miles. Our companions were an unembarrassed woman with pendulous breasts and stretch marks, a five-year-old kid with his little penis waggling like an acorn on a stem, a hairy-backed guy with a bandanna. They lived in the hills and came down here for baths. I glanced at the ridgelines. Somewhere out there were cabins, yurts, tipis. People lived like this all the time, not suburban runaways like us on a lark, escapees from the military discipline of Outward Bound, but people who had chosen another way. Who didn't give a shit about Harvard.

In my parents' den, Kim and I reunited after a month's separation. How could I have forgotten how tall he was, how handsome? His hair was streaked blonder from the sun, skin deeply tanned. My healthy beautiful Kim. Even the hairs on his arms, his knuckles radiated golden light. When we hugged I could smell a whiff of laundry soap from his navy blue T-shirt, and under it, an essence, familiar as my own skin, but exotic too. Kimness.

"I have something to tell you," I said, ready to confess an indiscretion, a one-night stand I'd had with an Outward Bound instructor after too much wine.

"Me too."

That surprised me. What did he have to tell me that he hadn't told me in those piles of letters? "You first," I said.

"Well, I was crossing the Cambridge Common one night and I met this girl and she took me to a party where I dropped acid. I've done it a couple of times since then."

"Acid. Wow." Kim had been having his own adventures. "What was it like?"

He smiled. "Amazing. Like Einstein's bit about riding on a beam of light . . ." He sat down in my father's big leather chair. "It twists your perspective."

"Did you sleep with her?"

"Yes." He shrugged.

A tremor of jealousy, fear. But relief too. Now it was okay that I'd slept with the Outward Bound instructor. I straddled Kim's lap. Pushed against the rumpled denim of his crotch and watched his eyes flicker, his breath catch. "Are you going to see her again?" I asked.

"No. Mmmmm . . . so what's your news?"

I started to shape the words about the instructor but realized then that it didn't matter. We were voyagers, explorers. Whom we slept with wasn't the point. I drew in breath. "I don't want to go to college. I want to go out West. I want you to go with me." I hadn't known it until I said it, but it made so much sense. I wouldn't have to go to my third-choice college. Kim wouldn't have to work at the Lincoln-Mercury garage and live in that dumpy studio apartment with the roaches in downtown Boston. We would be free.

"Whoa! When did you decide this? What about your parents' deposit?"

I'd be gone and my father wouldn't be able to do much about it. "Screw it. I'm sick of school. There's a lot of other stuff to learn. We can sell our ten-speeds," I said. "I bet I can get sixty bucks for mine."

"What about my lease?" He asked. "My job?"

"Is that the life you want?"

Kim gripped my hips, shifted me closer. "I want you," he said.

Before we left for Colorado, Kim's Malibu was stolen in Boston. I wanted to hitch, anyway. We'd learn more that way, I insisted. Though Kim wanted quiet time to write and an undemanding job, he let himself be pulled along by my enormous will, a will that had once been directed at starving, but now spun with a desire to consume the world.

We thumbed rides from Kim's parents' house as far as Vail. A fake Tyrolean ski village, Vail was gearing up for winter. Hammer blows rang out against the echoing mountainsides. A phony clock tower stood guard over the "town." New construction sprouted everywhere. Half-built ski condos and chalets crowded the hills across the highway. This wasn't where we'd meant to land, but it was getting on toward dusk and it was chilly at that altitude. We needed a place to sleep.

"You sit here," Kim motioned to a picnic table in front of a café, "and I'll disappear for a while."

We both understood he'd set me out as bait. I rested my red Kelty pack against the picnic table bench, sat cross-legged in my overalls, watching the tanned, trim ski bums and businessmen pass by. A poster taped to the café door announced a "Miss Vail" beauty contest that night at one of the bars. I wondered what Miss Vail would look like. Blonde, I bet.

"Hey, lady. You travelin'?" A barrel-chested longhair, sporting a striped railroad cap and a brown Fu Manchu mustache, stood before me. A large malamute wearing a neckerchief panted beside him.

I nodded.

"You need a place to stay?" He rocked back on his heels, flashed big gapped teeth.

"Uh-huh."

"Cool. You can crash with us, man."

I caught a glimpse of Kim's shirt around the edge of the café. "Is it okay I'm traveling with my boyfriend?"

"No problem. I'm Harry, and this," he gestured to the dog, "is Bumpkin."

Passing joints in the cab of his truck, Harry drove us to Minturn, a little railway town tucked into a narrow river valley several miles from Vail. The hills above Minturn were lower, the vegetation sparser. The ski boom hadn't yet spilled into the town. "Got to pick up my kid from the sitter," Harry announced, but first he took us to a railroad bar. I got tipsy quickly on my first taste of whiskey while the sun fell behind the sage-spotted hills and old railroad men hunched on their stools. Light shot through the dusty windows at an angle, illuminating a patch of floorboard, a ring of condensation on the bar. This was the real West, I thought. Not Vail. I squeezed Kim's knee. Things were falling into place.

Then we were in the pickup, Harry's toddler jouncing across our laps. I squinched my nose against the stink of dirty diaper. Harry parked in front of a small stucco bungalow. His wife took the child from his arms, gave us the once over. "I'm not cooking," she warned.

"No problem," Harry raised a greasy paper sack, "I'll cook."

Barbara was dark, sexy, intense, with long black hair and big, low slung breasts. I watched her lay the boy on the couch and change his diaper.

"Having a kid must be weird," I said.

She grimaced. "It's a trip." When the kid was changed, she lit up a joint and passed it to me. She had been driving an ice cream truck in Boston, met Harry at Northeastern, had to split that city scene. In the kitchen, Harry kept up a hooting patter while pork chops spattered in a cast-iron pan.

"Yeah, man, I was living in Alaska. Can't take this lower forty-eight shit. Alaska's where it's happening. No shit. They got some crazy people up there. Vietnam vets, misfits. I got to get back there soon . . ."

The boy slept, drooling, against a cushion on the floor. Bumpkin crunched pork bones. Harry talked, talked. "You got to have a scam, man. Everybody's got an angle. You know what I mean? Take you," he gestured the joint at Kim, "you got yourself a education . . ."

I flopped on a mattress on the floor, as Harry's voice went on and on. In the morning Harry took Kim with him to meet his boss on the cement crew. Barbara's business—selling sandwiches out of the back of a station wagon at job sites—didn't make enough to support another partner, she explained. She was generous, though, with her womanly wisdom: "If your period is late," she counseled, "fuck a lot, it'll bring it on."

I tried to get a job pumping gas, waitressing, but it wasn't season yet. Kim was hired on the concrete crew with Harry. There wasn't much for me to do besides wander Vail's artificial alleys, pace my boredom, cool my jets. Finally I hitched to Aspen one afternoon just to see it. Aspen played the mining town card instead of the fake Alps like Vail. It was glossier, redolent of bigger money, offering galleries and movie stars as well as pubs and ski shops. Art Garfunkle stood on a grassy green smiling to himself as people recognized him. When I approached, he screamed, "What do people want from me?" All I wanted was a ride back to Vail before it got dark.

I ended up on the highway. A vw bus stopped. Bailey, a short guy covered in grime and motor grease, offered me a place to stay in case I wanted to hitch back early in the morning. I agreed. In half an hour I was riding without a helmet on the back of Bailey's Honda 450 motorcycle up into the hills on jeep roads. I watched a hawk soar the valley below us. On a curve we spun out on gravel, tipping the bike, but I managed to land on my feet—where I figured I'd always land.

I slept with Bailey in his tiny camper on a platform bed that took up half the trailer. The sheets were dirty and Bailey, sitting cross-legged with his clothes off, looked froggy—thick body, skinny limbs. I wasn't attracted, but, according to the norms of 1972, sex seemed to go with the territory.

We were all like that back then, a friend says. Those same years she used to go up to Quebec with her guitar and meet men for a night, a weekend. Not all of us, surely, but a lot of us, were like that. What will my daughter think of me if she ever reads this?

Today, while I was making her school lunch and half-listening to National Public Radio, she overheard a story about teenage girls from Vermont led into prostitution in New York.

"What's that?" she asked. "Prosti—"

I've always presented her information based on the "need to know" principle—don't say anything until she asks. I'd hoped to keep her innocent longer but she'd already heard about sex from a playmate.

"Prostitutes have sex for money," I explained uncomfortably.

"But why would anyone do that?"

I tried to explain in general terms about drug addiction, people feeling bad about themselves.

"But if you don't want a baby why would anyone have sex?" she persisted. "It's just stupid."

I pulled her down on the couch beside me and started up on the "when two people love each other" theme, but I felt fraudulent. There are so many other reasons that people have sex and I wanted to protect her from all of them.

"I'm going to go out and play on the swings until it's time to go," she interrupted, jumping up from the couch. Thankfully, she'd heard enough for the moment.

In Bailey's cramped, grungy trailer, with the Moody Blues emanating from his reel to reel tape player, he started philosophizing about "finding his identity." The urge to escape came over me. I was hip to everyone else's clichés, if not my own. I hitched back to Vail in the morning with my lip swollen from Bailey's overly enthusiastic kisses. A guy who said he was twenty-five but looked ten years older drove me as far as Glenwood Springs. "I like intelligent chicks. It's hard for an eighteen-year-old to make it. You got to have friends, you know what I mean?" Another ride: a businessman from Denver enthralled with "mountain gypsy freaks." He sold them supplements for their macrobiotic diets. "I know where it's at," he kept saying while the Carpenters harmonized on his radio.

By eleven I was sitting on a wall watching Kim and Harry lug concrete. I wrote in my journal: "A whore takes money. I take freedom points."

Freedom points? What a harsh notation I made there at age eighteen, smug with false bravado. Freedom from what? Kim? My parents? My life as an AP good girl? Or was it just the times talking through my pen? In a childish aside, I wrote that I wished I could share my adventure with Kim.

Eyes red rimmed, moving in a drift of sleeplessness, hungover from beer and injury, Kim said that Harry had taken him to a party when it became clear I wasn't coming home. He'd slept with a girl there to get back at me but it made him feel worse. He wasn't interested in meaningless sex.

"Was she pretty?" I wanted to know.

"Yeah, she was pretty," Kim said. "That's not the point."

I turned away from Kim's pained face. *You don't own me*, I thought, with all the resentment due a parent rather than Kim, who was offering his heart. *You can't stop me. I've got things to learn.*

I don't know what I learned from the next guy, a pretty boy from San Francisco ("I hate when tourists call it *Frisco*," Steve sneered) who was piloting a drive-away vehicle to Virginia, where he was scheduled to join the marines in three days. I tried to picture him with a shaved scalp, a machine gun. "What do you want to join the marines for?" I asked. "You'll go to Vietnam."

He shrugged. "Got to go somewhere. You want to go somewhere with me tonight?"

I wasn't sure what had happened the next morning when Steve dumped me on the side of the highway in Boulder. A trick had been played on me; what had seemed like power—to hold a man's attention, to provoke his need—had turned to powerlessness. But I was hooked. If they wanted me at all, then I existed in the world.

After my sister let my mother know that I'd shown up at her Boulder dorm with a strange guy, my mother rebuked me over the phone. "I respect *my* body," she said. "Not like you."

Her comment left me puzzled. What was there to respect?

This time, when I came back, there was no discussion, just a tightening in Kim, as though he had to carry himself ever straighter to hold it in. How much he must have feared losing me to accept such behavior. Perhaps he feared for me, for my safety. As my surrogate parent, he kept extending the safety net.

Kim's parents called—a summons had come from the Selective Service. Kim was going to be drafted. Harry had a plan: we'd run off to Canada together. First we all headed to Kim's parents' house to get ready. So these were the consequences Kim had spoken of two years earlier. If he left his country to avoid the draft, he wouldn't get off scot-free, though I could come home at any time.

Gloria and John Janik, exceptionally tolerant or exceptionally fearful of conflict, never uttered a word of criticism as a house full of hippies with a diapered child bungled about stoned. They expressed no protest that their golden son was preparing to be a draft dodger. But then the Selective Service announced they'd only be calling up men whose draft lottery number was a few short of Kim's. We weren't moving to Canada after all. We stood in the Janik's driveway blearily waving as Harry and his crew pulled out in the pickup, headed for Canada anyway. The Colorado sun blazed on the ranch house rooftops. The flat plains town stretched forth in a grid of lots and glaring sidewalks. I wanted to head west again.

Kim bought a decrepit beige Corvair van and we returned to Vail, where he hoped to get his cement job back. We moved into Harry's Minturn bungalow but we couldn't make the rent. When we left I took a pair of filigree Indian earrings that Barbara had forgotten on the windowsill. They still lie in the bottom of my jewelry box, a cheap and flimsy reminder.

Why would I want to be reminded of a chunk of my history that turned out desperate and sordid? For me, all past events take on a patina. I hoard all memories, even ugly ones. I insist on their value, turn junk into expensive antique. I crave continuity no matter the story. Perhaps we all long for our former selves, even if those selves were misguided or worse. It's still a loss, a self we'll never meet again, as much a part of us—and as disconnected from us—as a first love. I don't miss eighteen-year-old Laurie whom I'd surely dislike if I met now, but sometimes I crave the newness of the world as it seemed to me then: the whole huge discoverable thrill of it. There were no limits to what might happen.

In Minturn, Kim found us a dingy two-room log cabin patched with sheet metal and lined with linoleum and fake wood paneling, set in the midst of sagging house trailers. Across the street, the Eagle River flowed. In the golden fall evenings, Kim snuck down to the river with his pole, hunched so that his shadow wouldn't scare the trout. I read paperbacks, fidgeted with boredom and a sense of being stalled. This wasn't what I'd had in mind. Harry had taken all the excitement with him. Why did Kim think he had to *work* when there were places to go, things to see? "I've got loans to pay off," Kim explained edgily. "I've got insurance for the van. I've got rent to pay."

I started selling slapped together sandwiches out of the Corvair at construction sites. At the enormous condo project where Kim lugged cement, a big-shouldered, slim-hipped carpenter named Chris and I exchanged glances. He had swooping dark center-parted hair and an easy California accent. He lived, he told me, on an old ranch outside of Eagle, thirty miles west. It sounded more exciting than a log shack in a trailer park. If Kim noticed our flirtation he didn't say, just hunched his shoulders, bent to his work.

I left Kim a note when I hitched to Eagle. I was gone for weeks. Chris and his housemates, an angry Polish kid from Chicago only a few months back from Vietnam, and a vague, pudgy boy from Chris's California hometown, agreed to pay me five bucks each a week to cook and clean in a house with no running water. The veteran complained that Chris was getting "other services."

Chris and I slept in a log bunkhouse decorated with antlers and Indian blankets. The first Sunday he drove me into the mountains, high enough so that the sage gave way to aspens. He said, "You talk too much, you talk too eastern. You pronounce everything so pre-cise-ly." I hadn't known precision was a flaw.

From the tilting frame house covered in asphalt brick, bare white hills stood out across the valley, eroded into lightning fork creases. Sagebrush flats edged into knolls spotted with twisted cedar. I was alone all day while Chris and his housemates worked in Vail. A gypsum-filled creek ran behind the house. I scraped eggs in the cold water. I played the same few records over and over: The Grateful Dead, and Judy Collins singing "Who Knows Where the Time Goes." The music spoke to some longing I couldn't name, a life I was almost but not quite living. The Dead's plaintive ballads and Judy Collins's song about a young man who rode the rodeo voiced a West that was almost in reach. I wanted to step into that black and white old-timey

photo on the Dead album, men standing in front of western buildings, to grab onto something that had already passed. I didn't stop
to think that the men in the photo were acid-head musicians tricked
out in costumes; they weren't living it either.

Friends of Chris lived in Eagle, two brothers and one girlfriend, Cal-
ifornians who decorated their shack with an ancient Texaco sign, Indian bedspreads, and old crates with lush fruit company labels. The girlfriend sliced an avocado for me, the first one I'd tasted, and scooped
out the pale green flesh. Its subtle flavor was as elusive as the secret
knowledge about how to live I was certain she possessed.

At the "ranch," magpies squawked and swooped into the dog food
bowl. I dug through a farmer's dump, fingered blue glass and tat-
tered letters. I found a single tiny, curled cowboy boot in the sage—
a rancher's long dead child? Hunters in jeeps roared through the yard
as I hid behind curtains. In the dry fields, starved deer lay stacked like
hay bales. I discovered a severed jackrabbit's leg bleeding on the living room rug. The dogs panted and howled.

I snooped through old letters sent by Chris's girlfriend back in
California. Christopher Wheat, she called him, an endearment that
tugged at me. I held photos, Chris in front of a swimming pool, leaning against a Camaro. I refused to think of Kim passing Chris on the
Vail job site. Kim shouldering cement. Kim alone in the dingy log cabin with torn linoleum, surrounded by trailers. Kim creeping down to
the river to fish.

The sagebrush sang to me in the long afternoons. I could feel its
acidlike vibrations. The wind shaped my name. It pulled me over the
parched land, into the cedar hills. I pushed through the pungent gray-
green tufts, over geometrically cracked soil. I wondered what would
happen if I just kept walking. I was mesmerized by the landscape. It
shrank me, stripped away my outsized will, exposing the part of me
that had always been seduced by nonexistence. The prairie wind blew
through me as though I were as brittle and yielding as the dried grasses flattened by its force.

Snow fell one morning. A surreal two-tone world, white on sage, little peaks on the gypsum creek. I called my mother collect and when
she answered I started crying. She said, "Nobody made you run away
out there. Nobody told you to stay."

Her voice diminished to a disapproving drone as I looked out the
window at snow capping the distant, eroded hills. Rock, snow. Noth-

ing could live here but sage and cedar. No wonder the farm had failed. If I stayed much longer I wouldn't make it either.

Only Kim could shape the world into sense again. When the boys went off to work, I hitched to Minturn. I was relieved to find Kim's pack, his books still in the cabin. I left some jottings from my journal, spacey, suicidal verses about "wild sage insanity" and "flying away quietly." I wrote a note: "If you care about me, come for me," though Kim didn't know where to find me. It was October 15, Kim's twenty-second birthday. I sat alone in the dingy cabin that I'd wanted so badly to escape, breathing in the safety of Kim's belongings—his folded jeans and a book open on the rickety kitchen table.

The next time I hitched down to Minturn, Kim was still asleep when I walked in the door. He lifted the covers, gestured me in. His knees fit perfectly behind mine, and his arms held the world from spinning.

"I'm sorry," I breathed into his shoulder, his neck. "It's you I love."

"Laurie, Laurie," he sighed.

Kim drove me to Eagle to pick up my things. On the way, he handed me an S&H green stamp stuck with a small cellophane square of blotter acid, a goodbye gift from Harry. It melted on my tongue. We crossed the river on a green iron bridge and the acid kicked in. As if summoned by a director, bellowing cattle with rolling eyes surrounded us. Dust flew. A cowboy on a horse spun and flashed a whip. Kim and I smiled at the lucky absurdity of having driven into a real-life cowboy movie.

The ranch house was empty. I played tour guide, pointing out the gypsum creek, the root cellar and farmer's dump. The sage rippled and swelled. Kim and I sat in the bunkhouse I shared with Chris. Kim's eyes spun cartoon circles, and a little bow tie bounced at his throat. He was comical, frightening. Then the antlers and jawbones stacked around the cabin became dancing skeletons. "I want to go home but I don't know where home is," I sobbed. My tears turned to big crystal chandelier glass, smashed on the bunkhouse floor. Outside, a jet flew overhead, dragging the sky in ripples behind it. Maybe the sky always rippled like that and I'd just never noticed. "Aren't you scared?" I asked Kim. "Aren't you scared, aren't you scared?"

"Scared of what?" Kim asked. "It's all just patterns." He was the rock, the firmament, the sky. Or a nodding clown in a bow tie.

Chris came home while we were gathering my stuff. He and Kim ignored each other. To me he said, "I knew if you'd run off from him like that it was only a matter of time before you'd do it to me." I shrugged at his accurate judgment. Chris didn't matter anymore—he wasn't even a real hippie; back home in California he drove a Camaro.

I could banish anyone, I told myself, though I kept running back to Kim. Kim couldn't banish me; eventually he exiled everyone else in his life, though I was the one who deserved it. He offered unconditional love and what I perceived as wisdom; I offered him an opportunity to be Mr. Rescue, as one old girlfriend called him. Perhaps I served as an illusory object of worship—after all, he was the son of a zealot. I also furnished proof of the unworthiness he felt at the pit of his soul.

Minturn again. While Kim fished I lay on a creaky cot and read *The Electric Kool Aid Acid Test*. That was it! That was what I had missed! Ken Kesey and his Merry Pranksters. So what if it all happened five years ago? I wanted to be on Kesey's bus where life was all spontaneity and invention. Where the motto was FURTHER. I wanted Kesey too, that charismatic father. He would tell me who to be.

I also wanted a dog. I picked up a shepherd mix puppy and named her Shawnee. When she wet the floor repeatedly, Kim beat her, shocking me with the force of his anger and his misplaced cruelty. I knew it was me he wanted to hit.

Kim drove me to Glenwood Springs to buy cheap supplies for my resumed lunch business. We cruised along the narrow two-lane road. The walls of Glenwood Canyon rose sheer to our right. To our left the land fell away; in the canyon's depths the Colorado River ran murky and green. I patted Shawnee at my feet. When I looked up, we were rushing toward the canyon wall, then spinning back across the highway. In strobelike images, shattered glass and asphalt raced up to my face. I glimpsed the greeny swirl of river far below as we flipped once, twice, and then I heard the whump as we settled onto a guardrail. Two feet to the left of our suspended fender, there was no rail. Kim was thrown into the back of the van. The puppy had jammed under the dashboard. When we climbed out, cars were already lined up, honking. "Shut up!" I screamed. "Shut up! Shut up! Shut up!" Cans of cheap soda rolled across the highway.

The van was judged a total loss and Kim was issued a ticket for negligent driving. "How did it happen?" I demanded. I couldn't believe that Kim could have screwed up like that. "It's the grass and the acid," I accused. "You're losing it."

"That wasn't it," Kim insisted. "I just overcorrected. A truck was coming toward us, over the line." We hitched back to Minturn with our dog. We had no vehicle anymore, no way for Kim to get to work, no sandwich business.

"I know," I announced. "Let's hitchhike to Oregon, to see Ken Kesey." So what if it was November now, and freezing?

Kim must have thought it a fool's errand, sure to blow up in his face if we ever did reach Kesey. Still, he gritted his teeth, bowed his head, complied.

Wyoming: the wind howled, brown grasses bent horizontal, antelope leaped across dead fields. My puppy shivered on her rope. Cowboys screamed from their pickups, gave us the finger. We slept in abandoned buildings with drunken squatters, or in the vans of other traveling longhairs. When we couldn't find someone to take us in, Kim spent his last dollars on a motel room in whatever dive we could walk to.

I paced the small rectangle: a sink on the wall with rust stains, yellowed blinds torn in one corner, dirt ground into the thin carpet, a tilting dresser. Kim was in the bathroom. I laced my boots, stuffed my belongings back into the pack. Outside the wind wailed. What was taking so long? I needed to be moving, moving, moving. Two strong impulses kept me running—the hunger to discover, the desire to flee. All Albertses are frantic with impatience; all of us have spent much of our lives running from ourselves. My father can put fifty thousand miles a year on a car just to keep moving; my sister fills all dead time with logistical details; my brother works seventy hours a week. My mother, even while enduring radiation therapy, won't miss an art opening or a concert—anything not to stay home. Motion is our first drug. In this second life, the quiet one I've been granted, to endure a child's lolling pace is still a strenuous test of my will.

"Hey," I called to Kim, "let's get going."

"Laurie," Kim's voice was muffled behind the bathroom door. "I'd like to take a shit in peace, if you don't mind."

"Well do you have to be so slow about it?" I could have been my father, fuming at my mother for sipping coffee—*he* threw cold water into his tea so as not to waste time—or berating one of his kids for being too slow tying a shoe.

"Yes I DO!" Kim shouted back.

"Well *excuse* me. What are you doing in there, anyway? Writing poems? I was ready half an hour ago. You aren't even packed."

The sound of flushing. Kim came out and started arranging things carefully into his pack. "God, do you always have to be so meticulous?" I complained.

"Jesus Christ!" Kim pitched a pair of socks across the room. The puppy whined fearfully. "Do you have to be such a bitch? What's the rush? Where do you even think you're going?" Kim sat down on the bed, its bad springs sinking. His face looked ashy, drained. "Look, Laurie," he said, "why don't you just go on out there by yourself and I'll head back to Morrissey? You don't need me as your chaperone."

"No!" I didn't want to stand out there alone in that wind, with the hippie-hating cowboys leering. "No, I *do* want you with me. I do. I *need* you with me. Please. Please."

"Laurie," he said, "what's happening to you?"

"Nothing." I could feel the blood jittering in my veins as though I were pumped with speed, the meanness taking hold. "I just want to get going." I had no idea what was happening to me, only that I had to *move*.

Kim picked up the socks he'd thrown and placed them neatly in his pack. "This is bullshit," he muttered.

We got stuck walking across lava fields in Craters of the Moon, Idaho. Checked by cops relentlessly. Everyone looking to see if I was eighteen, legal, or a runaway. And still I insisted we push on. In Eugene, Oregon, a pretty town of bricked pedestrian paths and bountiful bookstores, I looked up Ken Kesey's number at a pay phone. I started to dial but it hit me: Ken Kesey didn't want to know me. He was just farming out there somewhere. It was over. The Pranksters were over. The whole trip was stupid.

While we waited for a ride on the side of an Arizona highway, a trooper going the other way turned around and headed for us. We'd dropped acid half an hour ago. Kim coolly buried our dope under some rocks. As always, the cop wanted to see my ID. It was bad acid, laced with a lot of speed, and I went into a frenzy of searching through my red pack, throwing my belongings all over the ground. Kim chatted genially with the trooper, who warned us of the dangers of hitching and finally drove off. I sat down on my pack and watched my fingers tremble. I no longer knew why I'd dragged us out here. The trip had no purpose. I had no purpose. Big balls of tumbleweed flew across the highway. I was tumbleweed. Everything that had made up my life had crumpled, and I was nothing but a hollow tangle beating against a barbed wire fence.

Back in my parents' house my tiny anorexia clothes hung in my closet as though waiting a return to what I still thought was my real life: perfect Laurie with everything under control. This stoned, bedraggled Laurie was a stranger. When I stepped away from the straw house I'd grown up in, it was I who had blown away with the wind.

Friday Dec. 17, 1971

> *On this day I thee wed*
> *I join my self with thee*
> *On this day let it be proclaimed that*
> *As long as love shall hold us bound*
> *I am your friend, your lover*
> *together and apart*
> *in passion and in anger*
> *in joy and sorrow*
> *I am a part of you as you*
> *are a part of me*
> *and our love shall be*
> *forever entwined forever flowing*
> *in the energies of the universe.*

I wrote this hokey and noncommittal, yet momentarily heartfelt, vow a few days after I sat in the backseat of the sedan we'd borrowed from Kim's father, sneakily rubbing a hitchhiker's crotch. I could feel the hitcher's erection under his jeans, while Kim, spinning with headlights and sleepless on amphetamines, drove us from Denver to Boston. I couldn't stop myself. Kim's love wasn't enough. I had to provoke a reaction from every man now; if not I'd disappear. I had to do it, just as Kim had to love me. As later he would have to drink.

Rubbing, I looked into the rearview mirror, waiting for Kim to catch me, begging him to catch me so I could be punished or forced to stop. How scared and puzzled that hitchhiker must have been, wondering when the car would veer to the curb and he'd be dragged out.

I was like a kid desperately pushing for limits, but there was hatred in my actions too—how far did I have to go before Kim hit me, left me, proved himself my enemy, not worthy of trust? He was my substitute parent; I clung to him and punished him, expecting no better—despite the evidence—than I expected of them.

"You better keep that dog tied up," my father warned the evening Kim and I arrived from Colorado. "She'll get run over." His request wasn't unreasonable; our family dog had been run over in front of the house on busy Massachusetts Avenue.

"I won't," I said. We faced off in the hall of the "finished" basement where Kim was assigned to sleep. Behind a closed door lay my father's workshop. Half-empty paint cans, power tools, nail jars spilled across his workbench. My father, who demanded from us absolute order, lived in secret disarray.

"You keep her tied," he ordered, voice rising.

"I'm not going to. It's better to have a short life than live like a prisoner!" Neither of us was talking about dogs anymore.

My father swelled with frustration. How well I knew that red face, neck cords bulging. "Get out!" he ordered. "You can't disobey me in my house! I want you out before I get home tomorrow!"

"Fine," I said, spinning away. My father had to kick me out, just as I had to defy him. If I didn't, I'd disappear. I hear the echo of that earlier line, my fear that if I didn't provoke a man's desire I'd disappear. Provocation/defiance—it's a connection that makes me uneasy. I'd like to see them as two sides to the same innocent coin: requests to be acknowledged, made real. But there's more: in my twenties I drove past men at work sites, staring, demanding they meet my gaze. And when they looked, I'd narrow my eyes: Fuckers. Provocation, defiance, fury. That was my little brew.

As predicted, the dog got run over the next day. Kim and I dropped acid while burying her—I wanted, I told him, to see where she'd gone. Later Kim drove me to a dentist appointment. Head pinned to the plastic seat, I watched my reflection multiply a hundredfold in Doctor Brilliant's glittering tools as the drug kicked in. Back in my mother's kitchen window, rusty sunset clouds contrasted eerily with a steely winter sky. I turned to my mother. "I don't even know you," I said.

"Of course you do," she replied. "Just look at my face. Look at my eyes."

I did, searching for something familiar, just as I'd done when I was little and ran to her with a panic attack, afraid I wasn't real. But her eyes were flat gel, uninhabited planets. I retreated to my bedroom, where I watched the olive and rust and mustard pattern of my hated wallpaper pulsate beyond my pillow. My father came into my room crying, the second time I'd ever seen him weep.

"I'm sorry," he mumbled.

Sorry? Sorry? Oh, the dog . . . but that was a long time ago, in some other life. He could feel sorry only for a dog, I thought; the Albertses like animals better than people. I was too far gone to realize he was crying for us both.

At the kitchen table, I watched with fascination as spaghetti writhed on my plate like a nest of snakes. Didn't anyone notice?

After supper, my father summoned Kim to the dining room, where, as usual, he'd eaten alone. As a conciliatory act he decided to advise Kim about retrieving his security deposit from the Boston slumlord who had kept it in September. I lurked about in the hallway as my father's voice droned on and on. I saw the pewter sconces vibrating on the flocked dining room wall and wondered how Kim managed this conversation.

"Could he tell?" I asked when Kim emerged.

Kim laughed. "I was concentrating pretty hard. Anyway, with your father, you don't have to talk. You just have to listen."

This evidence of Kim's regained mastery relieved me: he could deal with my father while tripping. But it wasn't enough to convince me to go with him when he had to return his father's car to Colorado by the end of the week. The dog's death had triggered some terror I'd ignored on all those highways. I'd become afraid of everything, even Kim. Still, in the icy driveway I clung to him as though he were leaving for the New World. For weeks, I stayed in my old bedroom. Newly scared of the dark, I kept a light on all night, stared at my ceiling. During the days I phoned colleges for applications, teachers for recommendations. College, I thought, might rescue me. I shaped an application essay to convince schools of my newfound maturity and desirability following my enriching months away from school. It wasn't easy considering that I could barely remember the beginning of a sentence by the time I got to the end of it.

"You sound different," my mother said. "Not as intelligent as you used to."

The grass, of course. The all day, every day grass. It made me stupid and made Kim untrustworthy. I wasn't sure what the acid did but I feared it had pushed me over some edge and had turned Kim into a stranger. As if to prove my new doubts, Kim wrote that on his drive back to Colorado he'd lost a wheel at eighty miles an hour. He'd had a flat earlier and I suspected he'd forgotten to tighten the lug nuts. The old Kim never would have done that. It was the sort of thing he held against his brother. Another sign of slippage in this new, frightening Kim.

He wrote from Morrissey:

December 29, 1971

This will perhaps be one of the more drab letters I've written in my drab mood at the prospect of actually finding a job and having to work as an alternative to which I have none too seriously considered a life of perfect crime whereby I would pose as *a health inspector whose duties would entail circulation among bank tellers choosing bills for bacteria measurements after which I would vanish without a clue to spend the rest of my life drinking wine on the Champs-Elysee and entertaining elegant ladies on second thought I'll drive a Coors truck if they'd hire me which they won't as neither will Coca-Cola Boulder Denver Trucking City Moving and Storage Weiker Storage and Transfer and various other organizations and institutions to which I've offered my talents but I persevere this afternoon when I apply for a position as resident counselor at CU where presumably my duties will be to advise in my infinite wisdom immature undergrads in their plans and preparation for the future in short to tell them the best way to achieve success, security and happiness in that order . . . just call me coach . . . and for this I'm to be paid $675 a month what the hell there's no snow in Steamboat anyway but the chances of being hired after being seen are small.*

Miss does Boston live or is your return imminent where when and for what reason will you do whatever you're going to do though I really mean to say will you occasionally share my bed in sweet wetness which I have sometimes missed if you need a little love the cost of which is simply your soul if you'll recognize it

I answered with accusations—about his forgetfulness, his focus on my body, his new prose style.

He responded:

> *I suppose, that my mind is not so scattered that I am incapable of writing more or less formal sentences. However there is a certain problem when writing carefully: I don't tend to be lucid so much as pedantic, not analytical so much as pompous. The reason, perhaps is that I've developed the fine art of bullshitting and now I find it nearly impossible to avoid without a complete change of style. Thus my apparent (and sometimes very real) incoherence.*
>
> *In any case, I feel too constricted to use complete and cohesive sentences, and punctuation forever seems to be getting in the way. When, however, the sentences can break and*

flow and when images can emerge and disappear easily, I feel more freedom in my writing, a better rhythm and, I think, a more accurate correspondence with what is actually going on in my head. . . .

again concerning my letters, that last letter I sent you offended you because it spoke only of your body, and true, it did. I made an effort in my writing to evoke some of the more sensuous (fleshly, let's say fleshly, because I like that word) aspects of our relationship. Perhaps, this is something which exists primarily in my own imagination and therefore I failed to evoke it in yours; but this, of course, is not a failure in writing. . . . And so to us. The fact is, Laurie, you have carved out a significant niche in my mind. The idea of never seeing you again is nearly impossible for I will always harbor the possibility of everything working out at some indeterminate time in the future. Also never will I be able to think of you with someone else without feeling hurt and in a strange way, a failure. Yet both of these I can accept without a major loss of self. My life, fortunately, rests upon a number of different underpinnings, and in that sense, I am as stable as I ever was. That I am not stable in such a way as to make you feel secure is unfortunate but unavoidable, for I feel that sort of stability has only to do with the extent to which I'm able to conform to the way you expect me to act and be. To the extent that I grow and change (and hopefully at 22 I am still growing and changing) and therefore deviate from your expectations, I have no choice but to appear unstable. To remain stable in this sense would mean stagnation and would not be fair to either of us. I would simply be an object contributing to your comfort. I don't expect this of you, Laurie, please don't expect it of me.

I want you to be here now. But only because you want to be, because I'm also a little loved; not only because you've no place else to go, or you want to ski, or you want to live in Colorado.

(On re/reading, the whole thing seems cold (too analytical?) And this time the failure is one of writing. I love you Laurie, very much.)

Kim

I am stunned now by the insight of this young man who, in his own words, hoped he was still growing at twenty-two. He was onto himself about his "bullshitty" serious style he'd developed for term papers at Harvard, a style he was struggling to relieve himself of through loosened syntax. And he was onto us. He had me pegged—not wanting to be an object contributing only to my comfort, wondering if the "fleshly" part of our relationship existed only in his mind—and he had himself pegged. I want to shout out, this was why I was so tied to him, why what I felt for Kim was more than selfishness. I admired his clarity and perception as much as I craved his devotion.

In the letter he asserted that his life rested on a number of different pinnings and he could accept the loss of me, or my being with someone else, without a major loss of self. Yet, eventually, he did suffer a major loss of self. His professed inability to give up on us, his harboring "the possibility of everything working out at some indeterminate time in the future" was as destructive an addiction as the booze. He had us pegged and then he ignored what he knew.

Despite my alternating bouts of clinginess and hostility, Kim sent poems and explications of his poems. In the peace and stability of his parents' home he was writing again, experimenting with styles, stealing from his literary icons, imitating what he admired. I was the only one to whom he showed this work, though I wasn't very responsive to his efforts. I didn't care about allusions to Odysseus and Telemachus or cryptic imitations of The Wasteland. Ancient dramas or modernist angst were nothing compared to my eighteen-year-old terror. I was like the mother in a Milan Kundera story who, when Czechoslovakia was invaded by Soviet tanks, worried only about having no one to pick the ripe pears off her pear tree. She saw the world as an enormous pear with tiny, antlike tanks crawling on it. I saw the world as an enormous chasm in which only I was in danger of falling.

What part of this was ordinary teen angst and ego, what part breakdown, it's hard to say. The past months had proved that I was failing miserably at leaving home; nor could I stay with my warring parents. Everyone I knew had left Lexington. And so, cadging a ride off a ride board, I headed west again in a crowded vw bug, to Kim.

March: Morrissey. Kim had already found us a tiny ranch house, a cheap rental because the living room was stacked with piles of Sheetrock. We furnished it with a couple of chairs, a mattress, and a card table. I baked whole wheat bread that wouldn't rise. I made granola. I'd become a vegetarian after we'd followed a cattle truck while hitching in Wyoming, and a cow had stared at us balefully through the slats for fifty miles. Like my father, I extended my compassion more easily to animals.

After the flush of reunion, Kim and I didn't have much to say to each other, or, rather, he had plenty to say about what he was reading, writing, thinking, but I was uninterested, soon restless, biding time as I'd been in the shack in Minturn. To fill the blank, we played poker every night. Kim tied flies, tightening deer hackle and feathers in the little metal clamp with its penislike head, readying himself for fishing. His father, who had taught Kim to fish, had stopped fishing once Colorado gave up its restricted season. Anticipation meant more to John Janik than the thing itself. I found this peculiar then, and still do. John, Gloria, Kim—all three were drawn to abstractions.

We both found jobs in Boulder, Kim on a hot tar roofing crew and I, lying about my ability to drive a standard shift, piloting a Kwik Lunch truck to construction sites. In my third encounter with mobile food service, I was to be part of a fleet of "Kwik Chicks" or "goodie girls," as the construction workers called us. Kim delivered us both to work in his father's retired '56 Chevy, the only car Kim could afford. He came home with tar stuck to his neck, his hands, under his nails, his forehead. It clung to his jeans and even the waistband of his underwear. It was nasty, hot, killing work.

My boss's daughter, an obese chain-smoker, took me out to learn my route. At lunch break she parked us at a highway pullout and treated me to an hour of confessions about her ex. "And another thing," she said, crushing a Winston into the truck's ashtray, "he always wanted to fuck me up the butt. He gave me hemorrhoids, the bastard!" She pulled a set of upper teeth from her mouth and set them on the dashboard. "He done thith to me too, then he tol' me I gave great gum jobth."

The working conditions weren't much better than the training. Each morning I had to pick rat-nibbled candy bars out of the supply boxes. At the sites, men flirted and stole food out of the other side of the truck as I made change. I smoked the joints that the workers gave me between stops, took ridiculous shortcuts across muddy fields, and got the truck stuck. My route was losing money. My boss admonished, "You aren't selling hard enough. You got to say, 'Hey boys, we got some mighty fine hot sandwiches in the back.'" I took home $55 a week.

Kim's magazines came to his parents' house: *Daedalus* and the *New York Review of Books*, *Scientific American*, and countless other publications. I was reassured by his cerebral interests, even if I no longer shared them. It didn't matter if I'd become intellectually lazy; Kim could do my thinking for me.

On an outing, we drove down Clear Creek Canyon, a narrow twist of tumbled boulders and silty creek beyond Denver. I pointed a finger at picnickers at a roadside turnout, shaped a gun, and made a child's explosive shooting noises: p'choo, p'choo, p'choo, knocking them dead. "You're a weird person," Kim said, shaking his head, but I heard delight in his voice. He'd think for me; I would do rage for him.

I stepped over Sheetrock in our living room, stared out the horizontal ranch house windows to the next ranch house, the next driveway. Why couldn't Kim understand that this deadly domestic life wasn't what I wanted? Why had he chosen Morrissey instead of lively Boulder, where the other Kwik Chicks lived? Boulder called to me, a siren song of possibilities, other lives more interesting than my own. Kim seemed satisfied in Morrissey. He had his parents close; he had me safely to himself each night even if it were only for another poker game. He had no protection, though, from the mustached carpenter on my route who invited me to stay with him in Boulder.

Kim arrived at the Kwik Lunch garage to drive me home from work. "I won't be coming with you," I said. His face—I want to avert my own at the memory. He stood there, tar gumming his waffle-weave thermal shirt and speckling his forehead. His mouth opened, but no words came out. He was silenced again by what should not have surprised him.

I have a photo of the transfer of my belongings from the faded blue '56 Chevy to Jim's turquoise pickup. In the picture, taken in front of my sister's University of Colorado dorm, Kim's head tilts down. His hair, pale and shoulder length, obscures his face. My mother snapped the shot, an unintentionally cruel commemoration. She was there with my brother on a spring vacation ski trip. Charlie shoulders my pack; Jim grins smugly, his arm resting on my shoulder. I squint at the camera, looking haggard for nineteen, perhaps aware that I'd soon be bored

with this affable barfly and the University of Colorado football players who shared his rental house.

Two weeks later, shamefaced, I called Gloria; the ranch house with
the Sheetrock had no phone. "Kim's moved to Boulder," she said.

Kim's new address was a little red clapboard house with a sharp
peak, a vestige of Victorian Boulder jammed between brick city buildings in an area known as The Hill, a ten-minute walk from Jim's. I stood
at the screen door, shading my eyes from the bright Colorado sun,
peering into the dimness. Somewhere inside, Dan Hicks and His Hot
Licks sang "Where's the Money?" I knocked.

"Who is it?" Kim called. His white long john top glowed from across
the room.

"It's me. Can I come in?"

"Laurie."

I cataloged all the shadings of that word—surprise, pleasure, re-
serve. Kim said he was home from work because he'd been blasted in
the face with hot tar and got his cornea injured; he had a script of De-
merol. He had to keep the lights off. Yes, it hurt like a bastard, but he
laughed when he said it. He showed no sign of pain. Even in the darkened room I could see that he was shockingly thin. Hard work and misery had whittled Kim from 180 to 145 pounds of tar-stained sinew. A
polite host, he gave me a tour. Kim's bedroom seemed no more than
a converted closet. It was barely wider than the shelf supported by
chains that served as his bed. Kim poured wine for me from a Mateus
bottle and we sat across from each other in the living room.

"One of the guys who lives here is a hell of a guitar player," Kim said.
"He's teaching me bottleneck blues." I wondered at this new Kim, living a social life in a hip house in the hippest neighborhood of Boulder. This was the Kim I wanted, the one who was interested in new ex-
periences, not just ideas in books. Why hadn't he wanted this when
we were stuck in Morrissey? I couldn't ask. There was a formality between us now; it would take time to wear it down.

I dropped by Kim's every day after work. Kim admitted, when
pressed, that he was seeing a woman named Sandy. He'd met her
while fishing up in the mountains. What was she like? I demanded. She
was blonde, she liked to draw, she drew well. I immediately bought a
sketchbook. I'd always drawn when I was a kid. I drew my boots, the
houseplants, Kim. No blonde with a charcoal pencil was going to

take *my* place. He gave up Sandy willingly, although I was still living in Jim's house. As though choreographed, Kim and I spun in our little dance.

We sat in Kim's living room in the late afternoon, drinking wine, cutting slices from a red waxed wheel of Gouda cheese. "You want some more?" Kim asked, tipping the bottle toward my glass. I held the thick green bottom of a Boone's Farm apple wine bottle on which someone had exercised a glass cutter. Kim lit a Kool. He smoked a pack a day now.

The unlocked front door swung open and a tall man wearing a floppy, wide-brimmed leather hat and a long leather coat stepped through. Three more men, dressed similarly, followed. One of them turned and locked the door, pulled down the shades. Kim and I sat motionless, as though watching a TV screen. The first man held a gun. "Somebody's going to die here today," he said.

"Anyone have a match?" I asked. A cigarette wavered in my hand.

One of the intruders grabbed Kim's Swiss army knife, which was lying, blade open, next to the cheese. He pocketed it. The others flipped open drawers, cupboards. When they stomped upstairs Kim followed them.

"Wait," I heard him call out in his calm, reasonable voice, "you can't just go around taking people's things." I waited for the scuffle. The shot. Then they were all traipsing back downstairs, boots heavy on the treads.

"Can I have my knife back?" Kim asked.

The one who had taken it tossed it to him and they left. In the silence, I suddenly heard the slide of Leo Kottke's guitar from the turntable, his croaking, plaintive voice.

"They found some money in a drawer in John's room," Kim said, "and they took it." He was more upset about not stopping the theft than about being threatened.

The cops laughed us out of the station. "Your drug sale went wrong, huh?" They wouldn't even write it up. Boulder was a major stop off point between the coasts for the drug trade. The murderous STP family (Boulder's own Mansons) ruled the canyons. Squatters camped in the city parks. Riots had recently broken out on The Hill over Nixon's bombings. To the cops we were hippie scum.

I worried that Kim's housemates would think he had stolen their money and concocted a story. But nobody found his tale unlikely. A guy who had lived in the house a few months ago had been dealing dope. I walked back to the carpenter's house shaken, scared of every stranger on the street. When I told Jim the story, he shrugged it off. "Big deal. Everybody gets ripped off. Don't be a baby."

That night I snuck out of Jim's bed and ran through the darkened Boulder streets, dodging shadows. I opened the small hinged window of Kim's first-floor bedroom and climbed through. He groaned, woke, made room for me on the narrow shelf.

"Can I stay here now?" I whispered. "Please?"

Kim held me until my teeth stopped chattering, my limbs no longer shook.

In the morning, Kim and I and John, the guitar player housemate, headed north in the '56 Chevy. John wore a ponytail and little round glasses that made him look thoughtful, and he rolled joints while Kim drove. I was dizzy with sleeplessness, and then stoned, stoned before we passed the miles of new developments set out in pavement and curbs, the prairie land chopped up, divided—on its way to becoming a solid strip of development from Colorado Springs to Fort Collins. Across the raw, graded earth I saw the bright shirts of the curb crews and wondered which Kwik Chick would be delivering their mighty fine hot sandwiches, their candy bars today.

Big white clouds puffed over the plains to the east. The dark mountains walled off the west. We might have been driving a fault line between continents. I was in danger of paranoia, fearing the way grass made my blood rush in my veins, my heartbeats thunder in my chest, my thoughts spin like a hamster wheel. Don't think, I warned myself. I pictured us from a long way off—me sitting between two men in the front seat of a funky old car, smoking joints and driving without destination. Kim's knee poking from his ripped jeans. John's green crushed velvet shirt. The ashtray studded with roaches. From that perspective we looked cool, characters in a movie. If I were watching this movie I might envy us.

John said, "Whoa! Check that out!"

The Giant Slide looming into view seemed inevitable in its unlikeliness. I'd never seen such a contraption—an enormous corrugated steel structure bent into waves. A staircase ran up its back.

Kim asked, "Anyone want to take a magic carpet ride?"

John broke into the Steppenwolf riff: "Why don't you come with me little girl . . ."

Laughter bubbled in my chest. The movie had shifted location. We parked and took our places in line with cowboys and mommies clamping the hands of their little kids. Up we climbed, up and up and up, toting burlap sacks. At the top we balanced over the vastness. Before our eyes the plains stretched two thousand miles to the ocean, the mountain drainages etched into them like a topo map. I sat down on my burlap sack. The cheap fiber slipped on the steel platform. Kim sat down beside me. I reached for him. Then we were flying, hysterical with happiness and grass.

That spring, my body, as though in protest for bad treatment, turned against me. At first it was just my glossy long hair breaking into dry limp threads. I blamed my unbalanced vegetarian diet. Then my joints, my lips, my fingers began to swell. Blotchy rashes blushed and receded across my skin. When my feet swelled, I could barely walk. I watched the swellings move through my hands like some peculiar science fiction gimmick: first one finger would stiffen and puff, then the swelling would recede from it and move on to the next. It would take forty-eight hours to finish. Where there was no room for expansion the pressure was so acute I fantasized cutting open my flesh. When it was my lips, my eyelids, I looked like a girl whose boyfriend had beaten her up.

"Probably rheumatoid arthritis. You'll be a cripple before you're thirty," one doctor announced. "Lupus," suggested another. "Erythema nodosum," a third said, but when I looked it up it only meant red swelling. I also carried a monolike virus, they said, and strep throat. Strangely, two thousand miles away, my little brother manifested similar symptoms. His joints flared and swelled; rashes reddened his skin. At sixteen, he began to imbibe the prescription steroids that would damage him for years.

Although our disease was diagnosed two years later at the Harvard Center for Blood Research as angio-edema, essentially an allergic reaction to our own antibodies that can be triggered by illness, injury, or stress, the research doctors were disappointed to discover that we had the acquired kind. Family history, not genes, linked our condition.

Over the years, my siblings and I have specialized in stress disorders. Charlie went on to develop crippling psoriatic arthritis, while my sister bled intestinally. Three shrinks have diagnosed me with post-traumatic stress disorder. I admit it's an appealing diagnosis. It provides drama, blame, and vindication. But I never fully believed them. I thought they bandied that term about too easily. It doesn't seem likely that I could suffer the same condition as torture victims and Vietnam vets. I accept, though, that my upbringing could precipitate a condition that attacks both body and mind, and wounds others in the process.

Applying as a repentant convert, and keeping my swellings a secret, I received a summer job as a low-level "sherpa" for Outward Bound. I relocated to Gunnison and Kim moved back in with his folks. Once I'd left, Boulder held no attraction for him. He preferred saving rent to pay his Harvard loans, eating his mother's meals, weeding her garden.

Kim visited me on weekends, chugging for five hours over the mountains in the poky and ridiculous converted milk truck that I'd convinced him to buy from one of his former housemates. It held a narrow bed and a kitchenette and was painted an ironic red, white, and blue. What had I thought that van would mean about us? That we were Easy Riders, free spirits unleashed on the road? Why did he do whatever I demanded? Is it possible that he could have shared an iota of that vision of himself—Kim as Peter Fonda—or were the underpinnings, on which he claimed his self depended, beginning to slip?

On Fourth of July weekend Kim climbed Rabbit Ears Pass, switch-backed past a gouged, blasted quarry, rolled into Gunnison. We drove the thirty miles north to Crested Butte, where we stumbled on an all day party. The sweetest of Victorian mining towns, not yet condo-ized despite its ski area, Crested Butte was a lively place. We stood on the sidewalk and watched a parade. On one float, a paean to Bachus, gowned goddesses fed grapes to a plump man in a toga. The short parade ran through town twice, finishing up with beeping and honking bulldozers and backhoes. We drank margaritas at a bar called Zapata's, shot pool, rubbed shoulders with cowboys and ski bums. Sheets of light dappled the streets and fireworks screamed and popped as we stumbled and laughed through the alleys. In the afternoon at another saloon, a gay bartender tried to pick up Kim when I went to the bathroom. My boyfriend was so attractive, I thought, even men wanted him. How could I love anyone else?

When I had a few days off from my Outward Bound job, I hiked and camped alone in the mountains. I traversed rotten, icy snowfields and crumbling talus slopes. I trudged over passes and set up my solo tent beside glacial lakes. I caught up with a coed patrol and with them summited fourteen-thousand-foot Capitol Peak, easing my way across a razor edge by the seat of my pants. I felt strong, accomplished, brave, vindicated of my past failure. But when the male instructors, even one I found repulsive, took turns climbing into my tent at night, I couldn't say no.

I no longer confused my behavior with power. Acting out, shrinks would call it, as though I were a thespian with a role that had to be performed every night, or a child who plays the same pretend game over and over. I didn't have the words yet by which to tell my story. And so I was compelled to live it.

Can I stop here now, stop the list of men I ran off with, slept with? The men whose windows I climbed out of, whom I left sleeping in the middle of the night because I couldn't bear to see their faces in the light? Must I recount them all? Who is to recount every time Kim drank too much, smashed a car, got belligerent? I know a few of those incidents, but others will slide by unmarked. Must my obsessions, indiscretions, adventures, and errors be numbered? I think of Susan Minot's story "Lust," a list of a teenage girl's lovers. By the end of the accounting, the girl has shriveled and vanished. I lived that story long past my girlhood. But Kim was the one diminished. The one who disappeared.

In the parking lot of a stadium in Boulder, a teenager puked up peyote buttons. People searched for their cars. Puddles filled the ruts; a rain shower had fallen during the New Riders of the Purple Sage concert and now a double rainbow stretched from the mountains to the plains. I glanced over Kim's shoulder, hoping to catch a glimpse of an instructor I'd developed a crush on. We'd gone to the concert with a bunch of Outward Bound staff.

Kim spun me around. "What's wrong with you, Laurie?" His reddened eyes searched mine. "Don't you see you're making a fool of yourself? And me? Everyone was laughing."

"What do you mean?"

"You weren't watching the concert, you weren't even facing the stage. You were trying to catch the eye of some guy who doesn't give a shit about you. Sitting there like an idiot with your head lolling."

"Fuck you."

Kim grabbed my shoulders, shook me hard. So this was it, huh? Would he hit me and prove himself my enemy? Could I push him past a point from which we would never return? When I met his eyes I saw not the rage I expected, but tears welling on his lids.

I called Kim from a pay phone in a stairwell at the college library. Lean-ing into the receiver, I tried to hear over the voices of kids laughing on the stairs above me.

"How's the term paper biz?" I asked.

"Better than slopping tar. There's one I'm doing for some cadet at the Air Force Academy on electromagnetic fields that's fun and I'm finishing one on Rousseau for a senior at CU."

"Sounds like Gary's keeping you busy." Gary was Kim's new boss. Kim had answered an ad in the *Denver Post* for professional writers. Gary's employees produced manuals, contracts, grant proposals, but the mainstay was term papers. It was all for a higher purpose, accord-ing to Gary; he was gathering capital to start a city magazine. Gary, who wasn't much older than Kim, had gone to Wesleyan. He valued

Kim's Harvard degree and his ability to churn out writing on any subject, overnight.

"How's school going?" Kim asked.

"Okay. I might drop Eighteenth-Century Lit; Captain Cook's *Voyag-
es of Discovery* is kind of boring but Post-War America is good. We're
getting into McCarthyism and blacklisting. Roy Cohn and Ring Lard-
ner Jr. are coming to our class next week."

"Together? That should be lively."

"Nah, one on Monday, one on Friday. And I love ecology. We spend
a lot of time tromping around in the woods. Did you know the reason
there's so many white pine forests in New England is that after the
Civil War when the men went west, the women couldn't hold down
the plows and so they let their fields go to pasture? Cows don't eat
white pine."

"So you're reading the history of the place through the vegetation?"

"Exactly. The professor's really cool. And guess what? This weekend I'm going hiking in the White Mountains with a bunch of friends.
One of my friends, Alec? His parents have a house near Mount Cho-
corua and we're all going to stay there. Alec's into photography; he's
teaching me about the darkroom."

"You're not in college to make friends!" Kim snapped. "You're there
to learn!"

"I am learning," I said, stung. I didn't get it. He'd had friends at college. Why didn't he want me to?

"I've got to go," Kim said. "I've got a meeting with Gary in Denver at
eight-thirty tomorrow morning, and I have to finish Rousseau . . ."

After we hung up I wept on the stairs overlooking the college art
gallery, which was between shows. Behind a two-story sheet of glass,
its blank white walls mirrored my emptiness. I could no more conceive of life without Kim than I could have imagined existing without
my mother when I was little. Homesick at sleep away camp, I had en-
visioned her dying in a car crash and wanted to die with her.

I understood that any friends I made, male friends, were a threat to
Kim, who couldn't trust me in his sight let alone two thousand miles
away. But these were *friends*. It was different now. Okay, in the first few
weeks at school I'd made some mistakes—a creepy literature professor who told me I was "too mature for boys my age"; a night with a
dorm neighbor who taught massage and offered to "practice" on me.

Then I made friends and settled into a relieved focus on schoolwork. When an Outward Bound instructor showed up—he was lonely, living off a trust fund at a family estate in Connecticut—I screeched at him to get lost. I finally had a life; I didn't need him to bring along the scent of my summer humiliation. I didn't need to sleep with people to have friends.

In Kim's parents' house at Christmas, we spoke of why China and Russia, both xenophobic, had developed so differently. Kim took my hands and placed them on the raised ridges of the topographical globe I had given him for Christmas. "Feel," he instructed. He guided my palms over the barrier of mountains ringing China, then swept them over the flat plains of Russia, open to the repeated invasions of the Mongol hordes and Western Europeans. Geography as history.

I loved him for this. I loved, too, the way Kim saw himself in historical terms, reassuringly insignificant when measured against the drift of continents or the clash of swords. They mattered more to him than the ways he earned a living, the food he ate, where he lived. Only his love of me pinned him to this moment.

Still, strange cracks appeared in the armor of his indifference. Kim showed me a résumé he made up for Gary's prospective clients

"It's good," I said, "but why did you put in that stuff about travel in Europe? You've never been to Europe."

"It looks better that way."

I was puzzled, dismayed. Most people who falsified a résumé would amplify their qualifications, not their sophistication.

Kim showed me an article he'd written about J. Robert Oppenheimer, with whom he'd developed a fascination. Kim quoted, "I am become Death the Destroyer," Oppenheimer's words when the bomb dropped. The article was rejected at one magazine; as far as I know, Kim never sent it out again.

He wrote countless poems though he no longer bothered to send them to me since he knew I wasn't interested. Still, from afar, he directed my reading: Pound's impossible *Guide to Kulcher.* Eliot's *The Four Quartets*. Despite my own course work, I made dutiful notes on three-by-five cards.

In the summer I joined Kim in Boulder, where he'd found us a dreary little basement sublet across the street from the University of Colorado campus. We were at strange biological odds that summer. Suffering another flare-up of swellings and my monolike virus, I slept eighteen or twenty hours a day. I slept so much I rarely ate; I lost twenty-four pounds. Perhaps my exhaustion was brought on by the strain of being a good-girl college student. Perhaps it was some sort of infantile regression in Kim's presence. In any case, I slept and slept and slept. Kim came in, lay down beside me, and woke me to his lust. We sweated together and then I sank back to my stupor.

Kim, however, had decided that sleep was a waste of time better occupied by reading and writing. He set his alarm so that he spent no more than three or four hours a night in bed. The lack of sleep aged him. I detected lines about his eyes, something hardening in his face, a certain eccentricity developing.

In the few hours I remained awake, I read Jacob Bronowski's *The Ascent of Man*, because Kim celebrated the opposable thumb. I studied my ecology textbooks. I modeled myself after Kim. I had no desire to chase men anymore. I was determined to be a scholar.

Kim was writing a Ph.D. dissertation for a hapless history student whose professors wanted to get rid of him. They had handed him over to Gary with cardboard boxes full of undigested research. Kim divided his day into Gary work and his own work, which seemed to mean reading and taking notes on everything.

Our social life consisted of dinner at the Janiks' and one visit from Andy Jacobs and his girlfriend, Marg, who were on their way to California, where Andy was to start grad school. Marg was a strapping blonde with short hair. She was a friend of Kim's old girlfriend Marilyn—the one who had ditched him for not being Jewish.

I came back into our basement apartment, cool and dark after the brightness of the city streets where I'd gone to a bookstore, a rare outing. Something was up. Andy was thrusting the phone at Kim.

"Go on, talk to her," Andy urged.

Marg sat with her legs thrown over the end of the couch.

"*Andy,*" Kim hissed.

"Who is it?" I asked Marg.

"Marilyn's living in Denver. Andy called her up."

"You waited until I left to call her," I accused Andy. "You're still trying to get Kim back with her. That is so fucked up."

"Calm down," Kim pleaded.

"You know," Andy remarked as they gathered their belongings, "you can really be a little bitch."

I didn't remind Andy of *that* little jewel-like interaction when we began to e-mail after Kim's death. He was right, of course; I *was* a little bitch, a very insecure one. It would be easy to think it was my fault that Kim and Andy drifted apart if not for the fact that Kim let all his other college friends slide. Another former Harvard friend, from Seattle, told me that Kim had helped him weather his own deep homesickness and hatred of Harvard and the dreary East Coast. They'd met as dishwashers in a Harvard cafeteria freshman year, two westerners cleaning up the slops of wealthier boys. He said that Kim, who struck him as kind and confident, had once stayed up all night explaining an entire semester of calculus when he was in danger of failing an important exam. Yet after graduation, the friendship, if not the affection, waned. When I called two years ago, he was celebrating his fiftieth birthday, a date Kim never lived to see.

I desired only one thing the summer of 1973, beyond recuperating in Kim's apartment. I wanted to do a solo hike in the Rockies as I'd done when I worked for Outward Bound. I needed to prove my own fortitude in the face of my dependence. Kim, on deadline for Gary, drove me the long hours through the mountains to Gunnison, on to Crested Butte, and farther north to Gothic on a road impassable in winter. He left me at the head of a hiking trail I had traveled with Outward Bound. He would pick me up on the other side of a range to the east, near Aspen, in five days' time. I had my maps, my compass, my determination.

I set up my tent at Copper Lake that night, a lovely alpine drainage surrounded by moonscape boulders. In the morning I started over the first pass. But nothing looked right. At the top of the pass, a porcupine chomped away on the direction sign. The pass itself and the trail leading east, which I remembered as a worn dirt path, were covered with snow. I had to step in melted and refrozen footsteps, struggling to keep my balance. Below the frozen footprints, the land dropped in an icy, snowy swoop. I had no ice ax to catch myself if I lost my balance; I would slide for hundreds of feet before crashing on the boulders below. Although the air was crisp, I was sweaty before I made it across.

Next I discovered that a creek I'd remembered as an easy rock hop had turned into a silty river raging with snowmelt. I'd have to wade through waist-deep roiling water with a forty-pound pack on my back. Which was worse, drowning here or returning across that icy hell walk, which by now would be more melted and more treacherous? While I pondered my dilemma, a silvery drift log at my feet transformed itself into an enormous gray snake. Its hideous, sinuous wriggling propelled me into the river. I was halfway across before I remembered to unhook the waist strap of my pack so that, if the current knocked me down, I'd have a chance of getting out from under its weight.

Shivering, soaked, I kept on, striding through an exquisite day of puffy white clouds, crystalline air, aspens quivering in the breeze. I passed through meadows of wildflowers, mossy banked streams, forests of Engelman spruce. The beauty added to the land's malevolence. An unrelenting buzz of terror like a cicada's drone filled my ears. Bears lurked behind every tree. Crazy mountain men with knives hid behind boulders, ready to slit my throat. Every step might mean another snake. I knew it was all in my mind, but my mind was a runaway train careening down a mountainside. After seven hours of sustained panic, I changed course, inadvertently following the path of my defection from Outward Bound two summers ago. When I hit a road I stuck out my thumb, called Kim from the first pay phone.

"Come get me," I wailed.

Kim sounded disgusted. "Laurie. I've got work to finish. This thesis is driving me nuts. Why'd you make such a big deal out of hiking alone if you couldn't do it? I don't feel like making that drive two days in a row."

"I'm sorry, I'm sorry," I pleaded. "It was really awful. There's too much snow. It was dangerous."

"Shit."

Waiting for hours at a campground above Aspen, I had plenty of time to ponder his anger—was it my failure to have courage, the annoyance of being interrupted, or the fact that I'd wanted to go without him that made him so mad?

My own panic seemed to go hand in hand with my connection to Kim. I couldn't be with him and not be his spoiled child. Years later I visited Kim and we went for a run. Though at the time I was jogging three to five miles a day, I could feel the energy drain from my cells in his presence. It wasn't long before I whined, I slowed. I stopped.

The rest of the summer in Boulder I remained docile, sleeping, reading, watching movies. I made no more efforts at independence. When I woke day or night, to pee, to drink water, Kim was always awake, upright on the couch, book and pencil in hand.

September 13, 1973

Laurie,

. . . You are a distraction, a subversive waiting to ambush my mind whenever I relax. You have spoiled me, your friends have spoiled me. I long for something more palpable than daydreams. Real people, I long for . . . do you believe this? I have not been able to reestablish the hermetic universe that I enjoyed last year, feeding upon itself for better or worse.

And yet I'm not unhappy. I'm intrigued. I imagine two people (or is it three—aha! a symbol say you esteemed and hysterical analysts) . . . again, I imagine two or three people in a cave surrounded by blackness, sealed off one from another by thick, gray darkness. Tensely, alertly they listen to one another breathe. They wait for the disturbance that will shatter their fragile equilibrium, attack them violently and plunge them into a new reality.

. . . they are like Alyosha Karamazov's devil. Rather, they are his devil, and their breathing is the saint for whom the devil waits. He waits for the disturbance, he waits for the saint to collapse into depravity. And the devil is confident for he knows that men long for disturbance . . . through the ministrations of the devil alone do we truly feel our lives.

Not bad, huh? Movement 2 of the Russian Orthodox Symphony in which God becomes familiar with the feel of the soil—and likes it. I'm beginning to realize that this is precisely the kind of letter you don't like. Don't grade it too harshly . . .

September 24, 1973

. . . do I think about you because I'm frustrated or am I frustrated because I start thinking about you? . . . I've been frustrated a lot lately. And I'll tell you why. You, yourself, described the situation perfectly in your visit to the fair: a surreal experience in which you pay 35 cents to watch the world's biggest horse

soak its feet. I feel like I've spent the last two weeks watching the world's biggest horse soak its feet. The difference, though, is that we stand at opposite ends of the spectrum (the horse and I). At least he knows that he's the biggest horse in the world and that must give him a certain satisfaction. He really doesn't have anything more important to worry about than soaking his feet.

Meanwhile, I'm adrift. There's this gigantic horse in front of me, soaking his feet. The tents are all around me like great bellows, they bulge and collapse and bulge again. Pieces of straw float past; faces bloom and disappear. A nose, a smile, a clown with a wart on his cheek tumbles by. Are you beginning to get the picture?

Well, neither am I. Obviously, it's just about time to go fishing.

Fishing! That's a good idea. I went last Wednesday: the sun and I conspired to capture the canyon. The stream was low. I got my feet wet, and later in the morning the sun was warm on my back. I even caught a few fish . . .

September 29, 1973

. . . I want to talk to you and listen to your mind going round and round. Of course, it's a selfish desire, too. I immerse myself in reading and writing. It excites me. It satisfies me except that I know there's someone out there I could be feeding my ideas to, someone I could be clashing with. A developing whirlwind of energy that I could tap if only . . .

And so, in a sense, I'm a predator. But I'm a friendly predator. I'll trade you a piece of my energy for yours, and that type of selfishness can't be all bad. Of course, there's always the hermetic seal. The strange Laurie, the puzzled Laurie who can't quite understand what's going on "out there" beyond the impermeable boundaries. . . . She senses only the isolation, the nagging doubt. If she slows down, the dark recesses begin to expand and she loses herself in their emptiness . . .

October 10, 1973

. . . It's somewhat appropriate that your letter should have come in with the season's first storm. . . . The day and your letter reinforced my mood: a brooding solitude and anticipation. Everything around me, the people, my own actions, are like echoes—or rather they act like echoes without making any sound. I am now a specter. A distance settles around me as I anticipate leaving. . . . Who is she, this woman? And what will you be to her when you get there? A weight, another pressure, a new wolf in the circle, driving her further away, beyond your reach . . .

October 26, 1973

. . . by deciding to come East I never intended to put you in a position of making major sacrifices or passing up important opportunities. If I wanted a woman who was willing to give up her life for me, I'd find one. Part of my love for you (probably a very large part of my love for you) is based on the fact that I know I'll never tame you. If I ever had any illusions about that, you took care of them long ago and anyway I doubt that I ever had them . . .

But that isn't the question. It's not a matter of whether or not you're willing to give up your life for me. You wouldn't and I wouldn't expect you to. The real question is whether or not you're willing to mix our lives together . . . this summer I started to believe it could be done. In September you said things like "I'm ready to be monogamous." Now I understand that coming from you this is a somewhat fragile assertion and always subject to future revisions. But the fact that you would say something like that at all is incredible. It seemed to be an indication of something new, something that had begun to gradually develop between us last year and this summer. A realization, an understanding, a feeling that we might be lovers after all and that what we had to offer one another was very important . . .

Unfortunately, the devil's advocate part of my mind is not being entirely cooperative and, try as I might, I can't seem to ignore an ominous doubt. Have I misjudged it all? Toward the end of last month little pieces started falling out of place in the most devious manner. In our telephone conversations there seemed to be an element lurking beneath the surface, something slippery and sinister that I couldn't quite grasp . . . this type of signal *always activates the primordial part of my mind that wants to clamp down, close out the human parts of the world, and pre-pare to start feeding exclusively on my own tissues. . . . Now if this sounds like I'm asking for reassurance, make no mistake about it, I am asking for reassurance. . . . What I want to know is, are you just a little scared and not quite sure what you're going to do with me (and I with you) when I get back there, or have you actually begun to have some fundamental doubts? To put it less formally, do I have a fighting chance to pull the thing off and establish myself as your man? . . .*

November 10, 1973

There's too much to say, too heavy a load to carry it all in a letter. You've hurt me in strange and interesting ways. When you told me you'd slept with Pat, I felt stripped and ashamed. Why? I'm not sure. There are so many questions, so many pos-sibilities . . . don't be frightened, Laurie, I am coming to you as a friend. Perhaps we aren't lovers anymore, and though I can't rid myself of all demands and expectations, I'll do my best to control them . . . it won't be easy now for me to pull back and let you reassess the situation. . . . But you and Pat are too im-portant. The love you have for one another is, by extension, a part of me, and I have to find out what that means. I'm on my way and, oh god, am I scared.

> *Love,*
> *Kim*

Reading Kim's letters, Tom says, "I can't believe Kim could write about his feelings so clearly, so thoroughly, when he was in the midst of it all." Tom's small admission of admiration for Kim relieves me. So I haven't spent all this time struggling with the memory of a man Tom could dismiss as a nobody.

The letters provide the perfect oscillating graph of Kim's and my relationship: Kim's concern for me, his fears, his sorrow, and his lu-natic hope. My cruel confusion. It's a kick in the chest to feel, now, a shred of what the letters—I—cost him. And, with all their tenderness and intelligence, the letters make me miss Kim. I have a photo I took of him shirtless, wearing cut-off jeans in his father's backyard. I run my fingers over the black and white impression of his powerful young man's body. So, wanting a dead man, I desert in my heart, if only for a moment, my husband of this present, real life. Because no one has talked to me like that since, or, no matter what pathology, loved me like that, nor will they.

1973–1980

I slopped my cereal at the kitchen table of our communal dorm apartment, our "mod" in Hampshire College parlance, short for modular housing. My friend Joanna sprawled on the couch with a visiting boyfriend, a handsome vagabond who would soon lose a leg falling under a train he was hopping. She lay her arm over his shoulder, her honey blonde hair drooping across his shirt. She was clingy when she had a guy.

"You have to awaken the grounds," Pat intoned in mock seriousness, pouring boiling water gingerly over the coffee in the Chemex filter. He smiled, a soft-spoken, pug-nosed Irish kid with a wild bush of ringlets held back in a ponytail. Our "romance" had burned out in a day or two, just an aberration between friends. I couldn't understand Kim's mention in his letter of Pat's and my "love." It was the same with Emile in high school. Kim couldn't imagine sex without love when I was involved.

Alec, my best college friend, a short, impish, curly haired scion of Hawaiian missionaries turned pineapple magnates ("they went to do good and did well"), was telling us about "ghost dope." A high school friend of his had been killed driving too fast. His grieving grandfather buried his grandson's marijuana stash in the backyard. Alec and another friend dug it up one night. It was still good.

Kim came down the stairs holding his glass of bourbon. He headed into the dark, windowless kitchen, opened the freezer, and cracked an ice cube tray. I heard the clink as the ice fell into his drink. I thought it cool to have a boyfriend who drank bourbon for breakfast.

"Hey, Kim," Pat said softly.

Kim said, "Morning."

Will, who had long stringy hair and was starting to bald, glanced up from a *New York Times* at Kim. "Why don't you take off that hat. It looks like a dunce cap," he said. It was a stupid-looking hat, a little canvas thing I got in Israel when I was fifteen, a Kibbutz hat. I suppose Kim wore it to hold his hair in place, still sensitive about his high forehead, the minor recession at his temples that never worsened.

"Because I don't want to," Kim answered Will coolly, pulling his hat down farther on his forehead. He headed outside with his drink to sit barefoot on our steps and smoke a cigarette. I carried my coffee out to sit beside Kim, but I propped the door open. I wanted to be inside, with my friends.

Kim's modest duffel bag took up too much room on my narrow floor. His books crowded mine on my desk. The single dorm bed was too small. He was polite but distant with my friends. I wanted him here and didn't. When he played pickup basketball in the court near our dorm, shirtless, glistening in the late fall sun, I was proud of the way he shared the ball, never hogging a shot. He was the ultimate team player. Watching, I loved him.

But alone with him, walking through a cut cornfield beside the campus, nothing felt right. The dried weeds, their veins and intricacies, and all the shades of beige and brown matched our leached out connection, some dried up version of us.

"You want me to leave," Kim said. He looked pale in the late afternoon light. "Just give me a few days to find a place." Underfoot the broken cornstalks rustled and crunched.

My father drove out from Boston, took me to lunch, and stared at my breasts. "Still screwing around with your teachers?" he asked.

Kim found a room in a house in nearby Belchertown and got a construction job in a working-class city beyond Northampton. We saw each other occasionally. He reported that he hung out with his co-workers, played on their softball team. As in Boulder, away from me he led a lively social life that made him more appealing in my eyes. When he started dating a girl on his softball team, I drew him back and he was glad enough to come.

I wanted parts of Kim, not all of him. He wanted me no matter what. We were awful for each other and couldn't leave each other alone. The noose tightened, slackened, tightened again, strangling us both.

My mother found Kim a better job. She had left home to go to college in Vermont (she never returned to her marriage) and was living in the caretaker cottage beside a white clapboard colonial house. Her landlord, Henry Huntley, ran a business that sent its employees to colleges and prep schools to teach packaged reading and study skills courses. Huntley loved Kim for his Harvard diploma and his look—the perfect WASP with his blond hair, wide shoulders, his corduroy sport jackets, his nice manners. My mother reported, "Henry said, 'You always know Kim will do the right thing.'"

"Don't you hate it?" I asked, glancing around Kim's latest cheap motel room near some campus he was working at. He'd set up his toaster oven, his cooler. The ice bucket was filled first and Kim held a glass of bourbon.

"Not at all. I've got everything I need. I can use the libraries and the gym wherever I teach. I can watch basketball. I only have to work four or five hours a day and no one bothers me. I get summers off, I can write and fish when I want to."

"But isn't the teaching boring? It's so repetitive."

Kim shrugged. "The study skills are interesting. It's all about showing people how to think, and I get to learn whatever they're studying in their classes. I've been finding out about Aboriginal dream songs and the Hawaiian influence in cowboy music this week."

"But if you like teaching, why don't you get a doctorate? Teach history or literature or something you love."

"Too much trouble," Kim said.

In one of his letters before the Pat incident, Kim had mentioned thinking about getting a Ph.D., but now he said he was only interested in having time for himself. I didn't know if it were true, or if he was giving in to what he'd also mentioned in his letters, the part of his mind that wanted to close out the human parts of the world. Just as I'd taught myself not to want in childhood, Kim was teaching himself not to strive. A Ph.D. program would require him to acknowledge mentors, would make him vulnerable to others' opinions and judgments. He said it would require him to specialize, and he preferred not to. He could direct his own studies just fine. Perhaps he could, but he was also making himself impenetrable.

We saw each other when Kim swung through town between schools. When he taught at a nearby college I visited him at his motel. Kim opened the door and as soon as I walked into the dim room with its floor-length curtains and the cheap pictures over the quilted queen-size beds, I knew.

"You fucked someone here," I said.

"The chambermaid," he admitted, smiling.

"How'd that happen?" I asked, my breath quick. I was immediately jealous, fearful, but I had no leg to stand on, no room for outrage. I'd made the rules. This was what we did now.

Kim shrugged. "She came in, I told her she was very attractive, I put my arms around her, she was willing . . ." I pictured the chambermaid as a blonde UMASS student and wondered what she saw when she looked at Kim, his tanned face glowing in the darkened room. Though he hadn't brought up the subject, he seemed smug, or perhaps he enjoyed my discomfort, any proof that I cared.

We fought about minor things. Every time we had to separate I started a fight. Otherwise it was too painful to extricate myself. I picked on him—his appearance, his motels, his speech, his job. He picked on me too—I wasn't serious enough about my studies. I didn't live in an orderly fashion. There was a correct way to do everything, a certain order, didn't I know? After one fight, I traced him up Vermont Route 7 to Middlebury in a vision-obliterating downpour, then cruised the town's motels until I found the one that looked cheap enough that Kim would stay there while he taught his course at Middlebury College. Though Kim wasn't in, the reception clerk confirmed

that I'd chosen correctly. I waited in my car in front of the motel until Kim pulled up in his red Toyota station wagon.

"I can find you anywhere," I said.

Christmas morning at my mother's little rented house in Vermont after
a great dumping of deep fluffy powder snow. Kim, my brother Charlie, and I headed up a path through the woods to the Pinnacle on
our cross-country skis. Kim and Charlie took turns breaking trail. We
slogged up and up, past maples and birches and great sloping shoulders of hemlocks pinned to the ground with snow. When we hit the
hemlock branches with our ski poles, they sprang free, dumping their
loads. Clouds of snow crystals hung in the air.

At the top the storm clouds were clearing. Exhilarated, our hearts
pumping, we admired the view. To the west, the mountains ran in
bluish waves, white ski runs scarring their slopes. Kim and Charlie
tossed snowballs over the precipice and then at each other, ducking
awkwardly on their skis. We headed down, picking up speed despite
the deep powder, falling and struggling to pull ourselves free, laughing, laughing.

Later we sat around my mother's woodstove with glasses of wine.
Charlie created, with scissors and tape, a mock Dewar's profile for
Squeaky Frohm, the attempted assassin of Gerald Ford and former
member of the Manson family: "Committed to social change. Quote:
'I can't believe the gun didn't go off!'"

Kim and Charlie talked about combustion engines and computers
and the Vladivostock Agreement. I leaned against Kim's denim knees
while he stroked my hair. We could live in Vermont together, I imagined,
maybe someday we'd start a bookstore or run a literary magazine.

I called Kim from an island in Alaska. I'd hitched and ridden trains
and ferries to see Alaska before the pipeline went in. Out the window
of a friend's kitchen the land fell away to the harbor, where the old
derelict riverboat I lived on was moored. I was in love with the fishing boats, the fog lifting, the great oblique northern light, the clatter
of rigging, and the bald eagles diving for fish guts. I was in love with
the bars where loggers stomped in their caulk boots and fishermen
taught me to shoot pool and bought all my drinks. I loved the stories
everyone told me, and being mistaken for Tlinget Indian. I loved the

entire Alexander Archipelago, its bays and coves and islands, and the salmon shimmering pink and green and blue as they were pulled from the water, then fading as they died on deck.

I wound the cord around my body. "I lost my fishing job," I told Kim. "The skipper's old girlfriend decided she wanted to come back aboard. I don't know what to do now. I don't want to work in the cannery or be a barmaid."

"You can come home," Kim said testily, as disapproving as any parent. "No one's making you stay there. You should be in school."

"I can't come home. I haven't learned enough yet."

Recently, the skipper who threw me off my first fishing boat nearly thirty years ago found me by e-mail. He now runs a charter business, taking tourists on fishing and wilderness tours. He asked me to check out his Web site and invited me to bring my family on a trip; he'd give me a discount. In the photos, happy, gray-haired, paunchy tourists soaked in hot springs and pulled glistening salmon from the sea. So that's who I am now, I thought, ruefully. A middle-aged tourist on a charter boat instead of the twenty-year-old girl who crewed and hitched rides between islands and got her own commercial license and fished for king salmon out of a twelve-foot skiff in the middle of Alaskan winter, convinced she could be a fisherman. The girl told by an old Alaskan wolf trapper in a bar one night, "I knew you were in trouble the first time I saw you." I have to fight against the romance of it, the glamorization of that turbulent past.

When Tom and I took our daughter to Ireland a few years ago, I was puzzled by how different it felt to move through a strange land with my family. I'm just traveling, I realized. I'm not seeking a new identity, as I used to, with all the excitement and misery and hope that entailed. I'm not looking for material. I'm just on vacation, like any tourist. While my daughter took a lesson on a pony, I rode Irish hunters over cross-country courses, trading the excitement of galloping over stone walls and ditches for the old thrill of going home with a stranger. Although emotional danger has lost its appeal, I still need an occasional adrenaline rush, that most satisfying of antidepressants.

My mother remembers, "Kim came to see me after he finished training teachers for Henry Huntley. We sat out on my deck. It was a lovely fall day. He was agitated and nervous and talking about you and he said, 'I don't know what she's looking for in Alaska. She's wasting her life.'"

I'm not sure what he expected of me. To be the academic he wasn't? To go to law school, as my father had at the age of forty-two and now wished me to? Kim couldn't see that I was pursuing the particular education I needed. Alaska had filled me with stories; I sat in my leaky, derelict riverboat scratching away in my notebook before heading up to the bars.

Kim studied methodically, chronologically. He followed Isaac Babel's dictum, handed down by Gorky: "You must know everything." But Kim believed it could all be found in books, in museums, removed from the mess of life. In New York, at the Metropolitan Museum of Art, he reveled in the headless, broken sculptures of classic Greece and the Temple of Dendur in the Egyptian wing.

"Don't you want to go there? To Greece, to Egypt? See the real places?" I asked.

"I don't need to," he replied.

I too wanted to know everything, but through my senses, my body, through the oily blood-smeared decks of an Alaskan fishing boat, or on a riverbank with a sightless 30-06 rifle slung over my shoulder, watching a cow moose and her calf swim toward me in morning fog. I wanted to smell it, fuck it, lie down in it forever. I wanted to be a fisherman. I wanted to be *something*. I didn't know that soon I would be pregnant by one of two men: a half-Chicano, half-Chinese heroin junkie and sometimes pimp from California, or a green-toothed local drunk. "I could make you a princess," Charlie Yee promised me. Arlen merely threatened to hit me for looking at other men.

"Who can make sense of this?" a friend asks. "Your hunger to know a place led to this?"

Not led to this, exactly, but coexisted with it. Hunger for knowledge, hunger for abuse. No, it wasn't the abuse I craved so much as the charge I got from surviving it. That familiar defiance—you can't touch me no matter what you do. And something else: I wanted to escape what I thought of as my "sheltered" life in Lexington, Massachusetts—as though money and education had protected me from my father's rages, my mother's depression, and occasional blows. I made no connections then between what had gone on in our house and what I sought. A heroin junkie, men who fought in bars, the sight of an old drunk named Flea lying on a dock in the rain, a beautiful Tlinget boy whose father had drowned fishing and who was in danger of doing the same—this, I thought, was *real* life, and in the midst of them all, on some precipice, I was sure I was alive.

I sat cross-legged on the back of a fishing tender, a converted tugboat, at sunset in Taku Inlet, riding the rubber bumper that extended past the stern. In the cabin the rest of the crew played cards. The wake streamed out in a perfect V inside the larger V of mountains on either side, the horizon a blend of sea, sky, darkening. Alone, lost in that curl behind the engine rumble, I thought, *This is the only peace.*

Back in Amherst, in restaurants, in pizza parlors, Kim and I carried a cribbage board to fill the empty waiting.

En route to Alaska again the next summer, I got off the bus in Denver to visit Kim, who was summering with his family. An excerpt from my journal, May 25, 1975, reads: "Why am I alive and consciously here only in the newest place, the arms of an unloved man? I'll never know a better man more worth loving, but I can't love Kim in my gut. I've never loved anyone in my gut, just wanted . . ."

It wasn't true. I *had* loved Kim, as much as a troubled sixteen-year-old can love. And it wouldn't stay true. Though I was already thirty-five when I met my husband, I was surprised that I could remain attracted to someone who wanted to be with me. I suppressed my panic by telling myself it was temporary; Tom couldn't be right for me. A carpenter who never went to college? (I knew how to pronounce Goethe, but he was the one who had read him.) A man who lived in a cabin without running water or electricity? After our first meeting, I said to myself, *Nice guy, but I never want to live like he does.* Still, he struck me as the most present person I'd ever met.

In our first months together I went through spasms of trying to force a breakup, voicing the usual clichés. "I need time to myself," I protested. "I need more space." We were on the lawn of the cabin he lived in, his grandfather's old sugarhouse, in a clearing under maples. "Okay," Tom said easily. "Let me know if you change your mind." He headed up a trail through the woods to his cousin's cabin. They planned to have breakfast at the Miss Bellows Falls Diner. I stood there, baffled. Wasn't he going to get anxious, grab on, attempt to hold me? With enormous relief I saw that he didn't require me to make him whole.

September 1976. I lay on a mattress on the hardwood floor of my rented room in a farmhouse in Putney, Vermont. My mother and I had done a do-si-do—she left town and I moved in after I graduated from college. On the phone, from a motel near whatever college at which he was teaching his study skills course, Kim said, "If you can't be faithful, I don't want to have anything to do with you anymore."

Beyond my window, a horse whuffled and I could hear grass being plucked, jaws grinding. I considered. It was the first ultimatum Kim had ever given me. "I can't promise," I said to Kim. "I'm sorry."

"That's it then," he said.

"Wait," I pleaded. "Don't just hang up."

"There's nothing more to say."

I waited one day, two days, and then Kim called me, backpedaling. The triumph I felt was mixed with uneasiness for us both. He would take me on any terms.

Kim drank all day now, a slow accumulation of ice in glasses, bourbon poured, yet he never seemed drunk. He calibrated a certain intake that would keep his edges smoothed yet permit him to function while I began to drink wildly at parties and bars, a habit I'd picked up in Alaska. I carried orders in a restaurant where one of the other waitresses, a single mother, hunched over dirty plates in the kitchen, gnawing on half-eaten steaks. I typed. I barmaided at a smoky basement club in Brattleboro. The whiskey helped me ignore the grasping, gawking men, the hooting fans drinking shots of tequila while Meatloaf hollered on stage. After the bars closed I drove the narrow, curving country roads too fast, seeing double. I became the girl who fell down at parties, who drove drunk, who went home with anyone. The balance between my instinct for life and my attraction to annihilation was tipping again.

Still, I wanted to know how everything worked. I lugged bricks and mixed mortar for a mason, worked on a maple sugaring crew. I rode the sledge with the collection tank behind a team of Belgian mares. Their toffee flanks heaved, their breath plumed in the frozen air. In the sugarhouse, in clouds of fragrant steam, I dipped a cup in the evaporator tray and made tea from boiling sap. Lying in a snow bank waiting for the sledge to return, I looked up at the leafless, purplish branches squeaking and scraping in the breeze, a twirl of blue sky and high March clouds more real than my life, and prayed to hold this image forever.

In summer I threw bales into a hay wagon, the scratch of timothy and orchard grass against my bare arms, the chaff prickling down my sweaty chest. I banged nails, carted boards, snapped chalk lines. I sat on the edge of a highway with burning eyes, while trucks roared by swirling trash, exhausted after an all-night fight with my current boyfriend, a Vietnam vet who had once been pre-med. Phil said, "Fear keeps you from learning." He spoke of stuffing pieces of a friend in a body bag and threw beer after beer down his throat. He pulled a dead bird from my car grill and said, "Weapons. When the toads cross the road in the spring to mate they die by the thousands; nobody even sees them, nobody even cares."

I wanted whatever Phil knew. I didn't realize that all he possessed was unprocessible information, as I did.

"Do you have to be drunk to have sex?" my next lover asked. A good question.

Kim and I sat at a table at an outdoor café near Faneuil Hall. I had barely left Vermont in two years and had driven to Boston to see Kim. I'd forgotten the world where people wore business suits instead of flannel shirts and carried briefcases, where coifed women clacked in heels across cobblestone and brick. The little shops of the nearby Italian North End seemed impossibly exotic with their hanging salamis and cheeses, their espresso pots and gelati. I swirled iced tea in my glass and quoted my soon-to-be-incarcerated veteran's assertion that cars were weapons. The words were hardly out of my mouth when a pigeon flew past our heads and smashed into the wall behind me. I stared down at the pink feet, clawed and curled, the broken neck.

"Is the building a weapon too?" Kim asked, smiling. "Where do you draw the line?"

I felt foolish. What had I been doing? My mind was dead, or at least dormant. I wanted to talk to Kim, I wanted his take on everything—history, politics, literature. I wanted him to stretch my mind, force me to think, carry me back to the smart Laurie, the girl with promise.

Kim drank his bourbon, taught his courses, lived in motels, read and wrote. Though he'd shown me, rather proudly, a poem he'd published in a small journal, he said that he didn't care about publication. That wasn't what mattered. He was now working on his version of the history of the world, which he called *Eddies in the Stream*, a title that conjured for me either a guy named Eddie in rubber waders or Hemingway's "Big Two-Hearted River," in which a psychically wounded former soldier feared fishing in the shadows.

Kim was interested in the small side whirlpools of civilization, the little eddies that spin off from the main current, places where flotsam gathers before it is swept away. He believed we were, as a culture, just an eddy, a small offshoot, unless we faced and overcame enormous challenges, though what they were I couldn't say. I never read his masterwork, never saw it as anything more than a box of hand-printed pages, his tiny, even script unwelcoming.

I asked Kim's brother for his writings, the notebooks found in the car, several times, but Matt, who first promised them to me, later backed off. I didn't pursue it. I was afraid of pestering Matt, seeming ghoulish. Perhaps I also feared they'd be incomprehensible gibberish, or worse yet, merely dull. Perhaps they were brilliant, at least before his mind weakened, but I still wouldn't have been interested.

As I remember, space travel seemed to function in Kim's work, an unpopular view in the Age of Ecology. We had to keep exploring or die, Kim believed; we had to follow some manifest destiny of the soul. He was the diehard westerner, refusing to believe in the closing of the Frontier. He who eventually limited his physical horizons to motel rooms and bars.

Could he have been happy in all those shabby motel rooms? Aside from the consequences of his drinking, had he found peace in his scholarly solitude, in his continual shuttling from place to place? Was my assumption that his life was empty just prejudice?

In *Songlines*, Bruce Chatwin questions and celebrates the human nomadic instinct, the seasonal urge to move to other pastures. He blames unhappiness on possessions and settlement. What then of wandering Kim and his drinking? In the Aboriginal case, the drinking is a result of the destruction of the nomadic life. The Aboriginals say that movement is the way a human creates his world, re-creates the Creation, singing the songlines as he walks. I try to fit this theory to Kim and his road life. But the nomads weren't hermits, they moved as a tribe, a clan, at least most of the time. Kim's nomadism (just the nature of the job, he insisted) complemented and increased his isolation, became a hedge against risks. What then of my nomadism—Alaska, Vermont, Cambridge, Iowa, Alaska again, New York, Russia nine times? Was it any less a hedge, any less alone? I want to protest that *I* was running toward, not away from, but it would be only partly true.

We were both obsessed with frontiers. Kim's were intellectual constructs, though he wished dearly for the chance to travel in space. My frontiers were the edges of this world, borders between countries, extreme places where the blur occurs between the sun going down in the west and coming up in the east. The thought of there being nowhere further to run to, no true West, plagued me.

I spent a month in Boulder with Kim, trying, absurdly, to be a couple once again. Of that time he wrote:

> *Sept. 26, 1979*
>
> *I couldn't let myself believe you'd come to Colorado until the moment you knocked on the door. I'd spent the last . . . what? three years, four years . . . training myself not to anticipate, not to imagine, not to plan.*
>
> *I'm still a little fuzzy. Six months ago I could have told you what would happen to the two of us. I would have said that we'd always be friends, that our friendship would always reflect the unique links and the unique weaknesses of our history, that we'd never solve the dilemma of being unwilling to live with one another and unable to live without. That might still be true, and perhaps it wouldn't be so bad. We're both a little weird, and we might do well to accept an around-the-corner theory of love.*
>
> *But on the other hand, maybe not. We were a little disappointed by the lack of spark in Boulder. Still, after all these years, we should be able to keep our perspective. Things like this don't signify. They prove nothing one way or the other. If anything we are, for the first time in years, facing new possibilities.*
>
> *And I do mean we. I have my defenses, you have yours. But it would be wrong to translate these defenses into questions of guilt or innocence. I think that, on the whole, we've both tried to be honest. In our efforts we've all too often ended up mistreating one another, but I don't find that surprising and I don't find it depressing. We've committed sins of uncertainty, not malice. It's hard to forge an alliance between love and truth with-*

*out in some way dulling the edge of the people involved—and
that's the problem we're suddenly facing again.*

*To be sure, the dilemma's compounded by the contrast in
our styles. I'm rigid and you're volatile. Big deal. We're neither
one of us extremists and in the long run the contrast could be
good for both of us. For a decade I've been calming you down;
for a decade you've been shaking me up; and despite this summer's disruptions, what I notice most between us is convergence.
A fitful, unfinished, but I think undeniable trend toward agreement on matters of love, land, people, and home.*

*Perhaps I might be wrong or I might be too late. Perhaps
you've decided it's not worth the trouble at the very moment
when I'm deciding it might be. In which case we'll go shooting
by one another again and settle into some new pattern of separation. I think it's safe to say that we'll continue somehow. If
nothing else, our love is at least resilient.*

> *Love,*
> *Kim*

Of course we settled into our new pattern of separation.

We continued to drink, each in our ways. Kim forged his alliance of
love and truth by dulling his own edges with bourbon, a steady drip
like an IV. My drinking was erratic, social, a means of fitting in. The
Iowa Writers Workshop was a drinking place. We hit the bars after
class. Over pitchers and whiskeys we performed postmortems on the
stories critiqued, and gossiped about who'd been driven to tears in
the classroom, which workshop superstar had gotten a story in the
Atlantic Monthly. Booze laved the tears, bolstered courage, convinced
us we were having fun.

In Iowa I went to a Halloween party with one date but ditched him
and left with another man. At six in the morning I walked home on
the Iowa City streets in blurred makeup and silky slip, the remains of
my French whore costume. November first, chilly and gray, the traffic
lights blinked off and on in the empty downtown intersections. I clat-
tered on brick, dazed, hungover, onto residential streets, past Ozzie
and Harriet corner mailboxes, parked station wagons, porches with
white railings. I'm bad, I thought, with bleary satisfaction. Bad.

Just as I alternated between survival and self-destruction, I wavered
between wanting to be the good girl from Lexington—the one Kim fell

in love with—and bad. There was no medium. I began to have black-outs. After drinking at a party or bar, I'd fall asleep and then wake a few hours later with an intense paranoia and self-hatred that began to feel like a physical poisoning. In the morass of ambition, competition, and intrigue that was the Iowa Writers Workshop, not knowing what I had done or said felt dangerous.

The culmination was a party I held for my then writing hero; students usually hosted parties for visiting writers. The Writer and I were in the crowded, smoky kitchen. He said, "I don't know if you can write but I can tell by your eyes you've got it all." I hadn't yet realized that writers should be read and not met. (Years later, when my first novel came out, I sent it to him. When I approached him at a reception after a reading in New York, The Writer praised my book. His wife, standing beside him, scoffed, "What? You never even read it.") At the party in my apartment I was talking to The Writer about Vietnam—"the helmets they wore," he was saying of helicopter pilots. "They could just push a button and bring down destruction wherever they looked . . ." and then it was dawn and I couldn't recall when the party ended. The codeine cough syrup in my medicine cabinet was gone along with the guests.

Kim skied in front of me, a tall figure in wool and down, weaving among trees on the edges of a Wisconsin college campus. I strained to catch up as he receded. The frigid air pinched my lungs, and my skis slid on the crusty snow. Then, around a thicket of pines, he stood waiting, puffing cold air, smiling with pinked cheeks. "These aren't the best conditions," he said, "but it's still fun."

I'd stopped to spend my birthday with him on my way back to Iowa after Christmas vacation. Kim was teaching there for a month, staying in another of his cheap, thin-walled motels. There wasn't much to do in the small industrial city; after a mediocre Mexican dinner we headed to the campus to see the only movie that was playing, *The Goodbye Girl*. I tucked my gloved hand into Kim's pocket as we walked the frigid campus paths. He reached in and squeezed it. When I skidded on a frozen puddle, he steadied me. We approached the auditorium build-ing. Behind glass doors, the lobby was packed with milling students.

"Good thing we didn't wait any longer," I said. "I hope it isn't sold out."

Kim hesitated at the door.

"C'mon," I urged.

Kim shook his head. A plume of condensation issued from his mouth. "I've changed my mind. I don't want to see it."

"Aw, come on, Kim, it's probably a stupid movie, but it's my birth-day and there's nothing else going on."

"No, I'll not go in there."

"What are you talking about?" I glanced back in at the eighteen- and twenty-year-olds, bundled in down, chatting beyond the glass doors. "What's the big deal? C'mon, it's freezing out here. Let's go in."

"No." He looked stricken.

"Fuck, Kim, it's my birthday, I want to see the stupid movie."

"I'll not do it."

"*I'll not?* Normal people say *I won't.*"

Kim turned and strode quickly toward the parking lot and his car. Through the glass I saw the auditorium doors opening, the crowd streaming in. I couldn't even see the movie alone; I'd left my purse at the motel. What was going on? Maybe he'd spotted some student he was having an affair with and he didn't want her to see us together. More frightening was the possibility that he couldn't bear to merge his public, teaching life with his private. He'd put things into catego-ries, into compartments, and it distressed him to mix them up. If stu-dents saw his other life he'd be too exposed; he'd lose his teaching authority, the false personality he'd begun to construct.

I blamed these changes on Kim's new work selling the study skills program to colleges on his way to and from his parents' house in Col-orado each spring and fall after the teaching season was over. It was hard to imagine him a salesman, glad-handing, making social noises, but apparently he was good at it.

Kim stopped by my apartment in Iowa, heading from East to West. Together we checked out an apartment that I wanted to rent the following semester. The current tenant, a classmate, was watching a baseball game in the living room as we looked about. Kim glanced in, asked the score, and when he heard it, clapped his hands in excitement. "YES!" he shouted. The classmate, one languid leg draped over a chair arm, gave Kim a withering stare.

"What do you think of Kim?" I asked my friend Kate after a visit.

"Well, he's very nice, but . . . he's the kind of person Stuart would make fun of." Her stepfather, Stuart, was a sharp-tongued movie producer.

"Why?" I asked.

"The way he talks, you know, about his job as 'We.'"

I knew what she meant. Kim spoke too often now in the first person plural, as though the business and he were one. And he'd begun to use stilted idioms such as "I'll not." His overuse of "indeed" and other forms of what he had termed his "bullshitty serious" locutions developed for term papers had long been a joke between us. But now even his rhythms had changed. He'd developed a false language to match his false persona. And he had rules now, always cast in the negative, repeated as though he were amused by the absurdity of my requests. "You know I don't go to parties, Laurie. You know I don't socialize." He'd smile, but who knew what that smile contained when he said, "I'm a boring person." I hated when he said it, fearing perhaps that it was true, or that he was forcing himself to be one.

He'd spend hours talking to me about the Alaska novel I was working on. I could feel him leaning forward, tense with interest, generous with his ideas, as our voices carried between my Iowa apartment and some motel room near whatever college he was stationed at.

"I feel bad that we only talk about my work now," I said.

"Don't. You aren't interested in my work, but it doesn't matter, since I'm interested in yours."

I tried to be attentive to his work—the creation of an expository writing program the company could market to colleges, for which Kim wrote the guide. But everything seemed rote to me: the principles by which the process of writing was broken into discrete components, the predictable results, meant to appeal to academic clients. There was an overly regulated quality to it all that worried me; it fit too well with the direction in which Kim was moving. I wonder now if it were more than the subject, the craft of writing that excited him in our discussions of my novel. Was he being a creative writer by proxy?

After my graduation, Kim found me a job teaching study skills full-time at a prep school in New York through a contact. (I'd taught a few courses for his company when I needed cash.) I had little desire to teach high school, but I wanted to move to a place as much unlike Iowa as possible. I got, through a classmate, a cheap summer sublet in Westbeth, the subsidized artists' building in the West Village. The studio apartment was rented to the widow of another Famous Writer. Part of the deal was taking care of her geriatric cat and its stinky litter box. When I pulled open the silverware drawer, roaches scuttled across the spoons and forks. Across the river in New Jersey, the Maxwell House sign dripped its neon drop from a cup day and night. The scent of burned coffee wafted through the windows. Below me, prostitutes vied for trade on the old Westside Highway. The females lifted their shirts, exposing their breasts in order to compete with the transvestite whores. Gay men masturbated one another on the splintered docks where I went to get a breath of cooler air. West Side rough trade bars like the Anvil were booming; AIDS was only a rumor still. The *Village Voice* ran an article on a new "gay cancer" that summer.

I loved the city spectacle—a place, E. B. White said, for people with few inner resources. I walked endlessly through different neighborhoods, entranced by the Madonna stuck with dollar bills in the Feast of San Gennaro parade or the dangling chickens and douche bag–like cuttlefish in the storefronts of Chinatown. I was saved from my depressions, and loneliness in a city in which I knew no one, by the exotic excitement of it all. I rode the D train out to Brighton Beach to practice my Russian, which I had studied at Iowa, by eavesdropping on the new immigrants. When the newness wore off, my depression returned.

"Visualize your mother," Beth said. She was my new therapist, the first since Dr. B. in high school. I found Beth in an ad on the back of the *Village Voice*. She was a Gestalt therapist, lesbian, and at thirty, only two years older than I. She combed her hair into unflattering Ted Koppel bangs, but her eyes were a steady blue.

I closed my eyes in the blank white office. I pictured my mother's face but it was turned away. I couldn't make her turn toward me, couldn't make her see me. That closed face came as revelation. She was the first mirror in which I'd sought my reflection. She had turned from me *before* I turned from her. Riding the subway downtown to meet Kim, I felt enormous relief and unusual calm.

Kim leaned against the entrance at Westbeth. "Interesting neighborhood you've got," he said.

"Did you get solicited?"

"Only ten times."

I laughed. I was happy, really happy, to see him. We rode the D train out to Brighton Beach and walked the boardwalk down to the tacky, peeling arcades and amusements of Coney Island, then back to the Russian shops. The air was cooler here with the ocean breeze. The expanse of ocean buoyed me, thrilled me with freedom from the city's enclosure. The flat hard beach was speckled with cigarette butts. Big Russian women with mighty arms rolled up their shirts to reveal barrel bellies; men stuck fragments of newspapers over their noses.

"Alyosha! Idi syuda!"

"Come here," I translated, excited to recognize a few words.

A group of skinny Russian kids awkwardly tossed an American football across the wet, low tide sand.

"They're not used to sports that require hands," Kim remarked. "They don't know how to throw a ball; they've grown up with soccer."

I was pleased by his observation. I'd been staring out at the same kids without noticing. We sat on a bench on the boardwalk, held hands, watched the parade of overdressed Russian women in high-heeled sandals, tough-looking men in polyester.

"Garrett . . . " Kim started.

"Who?"

"Gary—he's changed his name to Garrett. I guess he thinks it sounds classier. Garrett wants me to come out to Denver and work on a magazine. Apparently he's got the backing and is starting up."

"Wow. I always thought it was just talk. What kind of magazine?"

"He wants to do a Denver magazine like *Texas Monthly*. He wants me to be his managing editor. I told him I've never edited anything but term papers and I've sure as hell never managed anything, but for some strange reason he seems to think he can't do it without me."

"Are you going to do it?" It sounded a lot more interesting than what he was doing—even something to be proud of—but I didn't like the idea of Kim living so far away.

Kim shook his head. "I'm satisfied doing what I'm doing. Who knows if the magazine will even fly? But you've got to give Gary—I mean Garrett—credit for dreaming big."

We walked again. Behind a cyclone fence, ancient sun-baked Jews played shuffleboard at a private club. In a small Russian bistro the barkeep's wife gently removed a boardwalk splinter from my hand. "Spaci-ba," I thanked her, which generated a disjointed but eager Russian conversation as well as vodka, and pickles to munch on. She was pleased that my grandmother had come from Odessa, from which she and so many of the Brighton Beach Russians hailed.

Sunburned, tired, Kim and I leaned into each other on the subway home. Through the smeared glass, stations whizzed by, lights flashed, a sallow, solitary face from a platform streaked across my retinas. I loved Kim, loved him for his wisdom and tenderness, and for saving me from being alone on a subway clanking through the dark. Back at my dirty sublet, Kim and I made love. The peaceful day allowed me to grant Kim some access I usually denied him. While the cat yowled and scratched in its litter box, my body opened and opened and opened to Kim. It gave us both a dangerous hope.

Another boardwalk a few weeks later, this in New London, Connecticut, where the submarines from the naval base glided down the Thames River and past the beach. I spent a week there starting a study skills course for Kim that overlapped with one he was already teaching. When Kim arrived we went to the beach, where we had our photo taken in a booth. In the picture I sport billowy, permed curls and a sunburned nose. Kim smiles, but his eyes have gone strange in some way that I didn't notice at Brighton: flattened, sclerotic, weird. That evening he nuzzled me, rubbed Noxzema on my back, covered me with a body that, once again, I didn't want.

As a child I had craved my mother so deeply that every drawing I made was of a mother animal with its baby—a Noah's ark two-by-two of a different sort. My greatest fear beyond doubting my own existence was that she would die and leave me behind. The part of me that remains frozen is the part that fears loving her. She will never be able to see me as a separate person with needs distinct from her own, just as I was never able to see Kim.

More than anything, I've wanted to grant this to my child, that she be loved for herself and not as an extension or reflection of me. When she was so little I could put her on my bed with a pillow on each side while she napped, she had a toy made of red rubber concentric rings attached to each other. She grabbed and I would pull her to a sitting position. "Upsy daisy, good girl, you're so strong!" I encouraged, then lowered her down. She'd giggle and I'd repeat the process. My voice would sound cheery, but inside my head another voice recited, *Now I'm a mother playing with my baby. Is this what a mother does?*

When she was two, in New Mexico, we played in arroyos around the house as though they were sandboxes, sifting pink grains, building little houses of twigs. We stood by the Guadalupe River dipping long grasses, pretending to fish. I carried her on my back, hands under her bottom while she clung to my neck, yanked my ponytail. I could carry her forever like this, more easily than I could sit still to build twig houses, play hide and seek, just be there. I performed all the tasks gently—changed diapers, held her, crooned her to sleep with songs that included all her activities of the day—but often I felt a detachment, as though I were watching myself go through the motions. I wanted so much for this child to feel my presence, not my absence. Yet I also wanted to run away, to hide in my books, to fall away from this consciousness, this fear of not being able to love, this fear of not loving right.

It was enough with Tom to take rides on Vermont roads admiring old houses, enough to climb New Mexican mesas, to cross-country ski in dazzling brightness. Love is our bodies together, our sweat mingling, me laughing when he does wheelies on his mountain bike like a fourteen-year-old. Though he's privy to my thoughts (and I, sometimes, to his), he doesn't need to probe all of me, as Kim did.

I stand at the river and throw twigs with my tiny daughter. They swirl away under a tangle of willows and sage. I grip the back of Becky's jacket. "Not too near," I warn. The dogs wade in and are sucked downstream before making it across. They're off to chase jackrabbits and pretend to catch elk. And I am standing on this crumbling lip, warning, "Careful, honey," the love and desire to escape warring so powerfully they're like the river that wants to go down to the sea and wants to batter itself against these sandy banks.

My daughter and I paint and tie-dye and make animals from clay; we sew a teddy bear, stick ferns and leaves onto eggs, wrap them in scraps of panty hose and boil them in onion skins to make lacy patterns; we draw and weave and sculpt and string beads into curtains and necklaces. There's no end to the projects I offer. We read, cross-country ski together, ride horses, plant vegetables. We talk and chatter and lie piled together under a blanket on the couch. Yet, if she listens to an audio tape or watches *James and the Giant Peach* on video, I feel as though I've gotten away with something. There are no parameters for what is enough. I have no models and so must create that link—mother, child—anew each day.

New Mexico: Becky strapped to Tom's back, we stopped to watch a neighbor practice roping calves from his horse. The calves wore plastic horns on a headpiece fastened under their chin. "Now everyone can have his own set of horns," Tom observed, and I laughed. But I sometimes feel like those calves, wearing the artificial version of what nature is supposed to provide: ease in being a mother, a wife.

Some damages are never wholly corrected. At this age, I accept them, just as I accept that I probably will never stop shredding the skin around my cuticles to raw meat, chewing the insides of my cheeks, grinding my teeth into fragile shells, suffering nightmares. It isn't a bad deal. I've been granted a husband and daughter to love, a peaceful home. But it's easier to accept my damages than the ones I caused, or the harm Kim caused himself.

Step back, then, look at the girl who said, when Kim came to pick her up at the Kwik Lunch garage, *I'm not going home with you.* The one who asked him to move East then slept with a college dorm mate before he arrived. Nothing to do but take these pictures, put them in the album with the rest: the play dates, the homemade Halloween costumes—a chocolate chip cookie one year, Harry Potter the next. The mother, the father, the child sunburned, smiling on a beach in Costa Rica, the garden dug and planted, acts that make up a life.

Kim stood in his Vermont kitchen under hanging Swedish ivy and wandering Jew plants, chopping, chopping, every carrot and celery slice into perfectly even cubes. He was now running the Vermont office of the business. Henry Huntley had moved south to open another branch, and for the first time Kim had an apartment of his own for longer than a summer. It was in Brattleboro, on Prospect Street, a narrow woodsy road looking down on the city. Kim chose a top-floor apartment, he said, because he couldn't stand to have anyone walking over him.

I paced his apartment while he prepared dinner. Watching his methodical, precise motions drove me nuts. "You're still an old lady," I said, shaking my head. "You have to do everything exactly the same.

My God, what would happen if one carrot chunk was a millimeter bigger than another?" It was our old argument: he was too exacting, and I was too careless.

Kim continued his measured slicing. "The question is, why are you visiting an old lady?"

I paced into the living room. On a table sat a pomander ball, a dried orange studded with hundreds of cloves and topped with a cutesy bow.

"Where's this from?" I carried the shriveled orange into the kitchen. "It's not exactly your style."

"Oh, just a friend. A woman I see once in a while."

"Kind of tacky, isn't it?" I said meanly. "Is it just sex?"

"You don't really want to ask these questions, do you, Laurie? You don't want me asking you." Then, he added slyly, "She let me watch her pee in the shower."

"Ugh, that's disgusting. You find that sexy? Gross."

Kim shrugged, kept on chopping his minuscule vegetable cubes.

After supper, after his many trips to the freezer, where he kept his bottle of Jack Daniels, I climbed into bed beside him. Kim turned to me, began to run a hand over my breasts. I caught a fruity whiff of bourbon on his breath.

"Stop it," I protested. "I don't want to."

"Jesus, Laurie. What do you think when you come here and get in my bed? I'm human, you know." He turned his back to me.

"Why do I have to pay for affection with sex?" I demanded. "Can't we just cuddle or something?"

Kim rolled to face me. "You're satisfied by other men, not me," he said quietly.

I couldn't explain that it wasn't that they were better lovers. He was talented and generous in that department, it's just that I couldn't bear being *loved*. It felt so much like invasion. I actually preferred sex with people I didn't like. It was simpler, just sensation. *Give me your hand, I slide your finger between my lips*—I could get drunk on empty coupling, but with Kim I froze.

Still, we continued to get together. When he taught in nearby colleges or attended business conventions or simply visited in New York, Kim took me to museums and jazz clubs and restaurants. On the Lower East Side, we walked together through the noisy bazaar of Orchard

Street. Kim needed a suit and had enlisted me to help him find one at a good price. Awnings rolled up, and metal security grates scraped open in front of the schmatta shops. Purses hung in tiers from hooks, suitcases, undershirts, T-shirts, designer dresses DISCOUNT! DISCOUNT! DISCOUNT! Shoppers huddled around a three-card monte game set up on a cardboard box. I spun around at the occasional Russian voice. Inside a narrow rectangle in which the suits were mashed together so tightly you could barely slide them on the racks, an old Jewish haberdasher took Kim's measure. "You found yourself a handsome one," he told me, sliding the tape up Kim's inseam. "You better hang on to him."

In a comedy club, the short, kinky-haired performer sneered down from the stage at the crowd of drinkers on dates. "What about you?" he taunted Kim, who sat upright and silent beside me at the little table. I glanced around the smoky, crowded room. He couldn't mean Kim. We weren't even sitting up front. "Yeah, you. What are you, some kind of a Nazi?" His voice rose to a hysterical pitch. "Mr. Master Race? Hup Two Three Four everybody into the ovens!" Kim smiled gamely but I sensed his mortification. What was it about him that elicited such responses? They mistook his rigid shyness for insolence.

At a tourist restaurant in Little Italy, where some famous Mafia shoot-out supposedly took place, Kim signaled the waitress as soon as we sat down. "A double Jack Daniels," he ordered.

"Why does it have to be a double?" I chided. Was he afraid he might have to wait for the waitress to get back with his next one? "And why do you have to drink so much?" Lately, I'd begun counting his drinks.

"Laurie, it's no big deal. I like to drink. I like how it tastes."

Right.

Out on the sidewalk the sun had not yet set. Rain had fallen while we were eating; the light now was lovely, illuminating everything with unusual clarity, glancing off the buildings and the freshly washed street. Kim staggered, bumped into me. "*Kim*," I pleaded, alarmed because, although I'd staggered drunkenly through plenty of streets in the past, I'd never seen Kim out of control. Well, just once, when we drove to a county fair with my brother and Kim threatened to knock a cop "into tomorrow." I no longer drank like I had in Alaska or Iowa or Vermont. I couldn't bear the sleepless 3:00 A.M. despair and paranoia, the worsening toxic aftermath. I recognized that it sent me into a chemical spiral I might not escape.

Kim smiled, bemused and chagrined. "I miscalculated. I don't usually miscalculate."

I steadied him through the Manhattan streets.

Sometimes Kim spoke about women he met while he taught—a friend with whom he went to watch Jai Alai in Hartford; a psychologist he'd met in Maine who was helping him look at some things about himself. What these things were, he wouldn't say. Were these relationships serious? Would he get married? I smoothed my voice because I promised him nothing, and he owed me nothing, but I was scared. I couldn't bear to think of Kim shifting his allegiance away from me, even if it meant his being loved. I pictured these phantom women, suspected that he frustrated them by withholding commitment. Perhaps they longed for him the way I had longed for one man who'd told me, "I'm in love with a woman and you aren't her." But unlike the guys who looked away as soon as their pants were zipped, I assumed that Kim would be courteous, appreciative, generous with everything but his heart. When I asked, he replied, "I won't get married. I like doing things my own way too much."

Kim's sister was in high school. They played tennis and jogged and hiked together every summer. He said, "I have to wear ankle weights because Sue will whip my butt when I get back to Colorado if I don't get in shape." He was going to see that she got out of Colorado, came east for college. She was bright, a jock, interested in theater. He would teach her to have larger expectations than Morrissey allowed. He was furious when she dropped out of drama school in New York after a few days and returned home.

"Why are you so mad? It's her life," I said.

"She doesn't know what she's doing!" Kim stormed. The intensity of his disappointment worried me. He'd taken too great an interest, wanted to mold her as he'd tried to mold me. It mattered too much.

I moved, once the sublet ended, to a twelve-by-fourteen-foot maid's room with a shared bathroom on the roof of a posh building, a psychiatrist ghetto, on E. Sixty-eighth Street. It belonged to parents at the school where I taught, a venerable Episcopal academy. Kim arrived at my room one day with a scabby cut around his eye.

"What happened?" I asked.

Kim shrugged. "I was in a bar in Pittsburgh. A guy came up and accused me of looking at his woman. When I thought about what this guy's woman must look like, I couldn't help smiling. He smashed his glass into my eye."

"So what did you do?"

Kim shrugged. "I decked him."

I pictured Kim by day, in his herringbone suit, charming college provosts and deans; at night he sat in the kinds of bars where strangers broke a glass in your face. No worse than the Alaskan bars where I'd worked and gotten drunk, but I preferred to think of my barfly days as an interlude, while his had become a way of life.

Kim wouldn't sleep in my tiny room with the shared toilet down the hall. The first few visits he stayed in decent midtown hotels— one had a rooftop pool that delighted me, all that turquoise peace above the rumbling city—but eventually he settled on a seedy motel on Ninth Avenue in the forties, near Times Square. In his dark rented room with an air shaft view, I opened a wooden armoire; a bottle of Jack Daniels rolled inside. I closed it quickly as though it were a secret. In the morning we walked the littered streets in search of coffee. Two transvestites, tall, willowy black men in dresses, approached. They gave Kim a flirtatious glance, then one, nose in the air, scoffed at me, "Honey, I ain't studying no tuna fish." Forty-second Street: this was Kim's New York.

My mother, who had moved back to Vermont after I moved out, helped Kim find a new rental, a quirky little house up in a hay field near the Putney School. "It has a working fireplace," Kim showed me proudly. He also displayed the furnishings my mother helped him select, the first time in his life he'd bought any. A blond wooden dining table. Dhurrie rugs. A Swedish couch and chair.

Kim started a fire and smoke puffed back into the high-ceilinged living room.

"It's smoking, Kim," I said.

"No it isn't."

It was. Smoke leaked steadily back into the room. "There's a problem with the flue or something."

"No there isn't!" Kim insisted. He went to the kitchen to crack more ice, refill his bourbon glass, while smoke drifted over the couch, the armchair.

"Kim, what's the matter with you? Just douse the fire. The chimney doesn't work. It needs fixing."

"There is nothing wrong with it!" he shouted.

"I want to leave," I said.

"So leave."

"Aren't you going to give me a ride back to my mother's house?"

"Find your own way," Kim said.

A new bitterness toward me had crept in along with a drunken belligerence and refusal to acknowledge certain realities, even those as simple as a leaking chimney. The dangerous hope that had surfaced the night of our Brighton Beach trip, with its ardent lovemaking, had set Kim up for a stinging disappointment that I had easily shrugged off. When a new romance fizzled, I still called Kim late at night, hoping that he could rescue me, that I could love him this time. But he finally acknowledged *that* reality, and for the first time ever, he drew the line.

Dec. 15, 1981

Dear Laurie,

It's snowing to beat hell outside. I won't be able to take advantage since I have to be at Wesleyan tomorrow, but one thought leads to another, and I realize that I suffer from two plagues in my life. First, I always seem to be where the snow isn't, and second, I always seem to be where you are. About the former I can do nothing, but the latter . . .

I don't want to see you when you're in Vermont. For the last two days I have been thinking about our years together and I hear only echoes. I'm sorry.

Kim

Despite my shock, I knew it was long past due. And I was relieved to be disallowed further misbehavior. What had made Kim come to this change of heart after thirteen years? Another woman? But another woman wouldn't account for the coldness of this letter that wasn't signed "love." Something particularly thoughtless I'd said, an allusion to other men? Whatever I said, I doubt it could have been any worse than many past incidents, but Kim, with his new house and his new position managing the business, was finally trying to make a clean break.

I don't know if being cut off, perhaps irrevocably, from Kim, was connected to it, or if it was slushy gray winter in the city and a job I hated, but that winter, my first in New York, my depression deepened dangerously. I took to lying on top of the low wall rimming my rooftop. Bricks pressed against my back. The leaden sky above weighted me, as heavy as my worthless life. I'd stopped work on my novel, exhausted and discouraged by teaching study skills in a school full of spoiled kids, and paralyzed by the great self-consciousness that was the result of my two years at the Iowa Writers Workshop. Below me horns honked. Madison Avenue stretched south with stop and go cars like an undulating caterpillar of lights. I rolled to the edge and pondered the twelve-story drop below. It wouldn't be so hard to just roll farther. I could do it. I wanted to do it.

I rode the subways late, walked across Central Park in the dark. A friend spoke of my solo trips to Brighton Beach as "looking for Mr. Goodbar-sky."

"You have elements of borderline personality disorder," my therapist told me when I asked for a diagnosis. "Not the full syndrome, but elements—the self-destructiveness especially."

"But isn't that depression?" I asked.

She said, "I don't see depression as your primary manifestation."

"What, then?"

She replied, "Anger."

Later shrinks have discounted her borderline diagnosis, but the anger business cut uncomfortably close. Odd that I'd prefer to be thought of as self-destructive than to have someone see me as full of rage. As though to be a victim is honorable in comparison with being furious. Odd, too, that Kim's anger appeared only in the late stages of being drunk, and mostly it was directed at phantoms.

Could it have been an abandoned child's rage, not just desperation, that led me to keep calling Kim, prompting this response?

April 1, 1982

A SPECIAL MEMO TO ALL STOCKHOLDERS OF OSTRICH, INC., A BLACK-CHIP COMPANY LOCATED IN THIS COUNTRY (or some other)

Item 1

Our Board of Directors is pleased to announce that "The World's Most Improvable Man" has entered his final stage of *development. No further advice from the Suggestions and In-sinuations Department will be required.*

Item 2

In order to preserve an orderly market for this highly attrac-tive item, the Board has resolved to keep its dates of produc-tion, its mode of distribution, and the response of its delight-ed consumers strictly secret.

In handwriting, a softened Kim added:

Hi Kid,
I always enjoy talking with you, too. But as I said last week, and as far as I can tell now, nothing much has changed.
           Love, Kim

He still loved me, I knew it. Unable to respect his attempt to free himself, I persisted. He, unable to further suppress his ordinary kind-ness, wrote:

May 1, 1982

I know what would happen if we met today. We would immedi-ately be attracted to one another, would quickly fall in love, and after a few weeks discover that the gears don't mesh.

So we'd throw out the clutch and examine the gears. The gears look fine. Throw in the clutch. The gears don't mesh. Throw out the clutch. Examine the gears. Throw in the clutch. Throw out the clutch . . .

Pretty soon we're both exhausted and wondering why this fine machine should run so poorly. Unfortunately, we're also stubborn, so we persevere. In fact, we keep throwing the clutch in and out for—oh, let's say thirteen years, until suddenly someone pulls the brake and slams us both against the wind-shield.

Laurie, I don't know why it didn't work. (If I did, I would fix it!) We'll just have to nurse our bruises the best we can. I love you too, kid. It seems there's nothing either one of us can do about that. Right now we are a distraction to one anoth-er. But that means we must each have something to offer the

other. At some point I suspect we'll be able to do that com-
fortably again.
                    Love,
                    Kim

Visiting my mother in Vermont that summer, I borrowed her car
and drove aimless country miles. The maples and birches hung heavy
with summer leaves. Everything seemed trapped by the heat. Eventually, I could no longer keep my foot to the gas pedal. I let the car
drift off the road into a pullout. I couldn't move; this heaviness, this
purposelessness had pulled me under. How was it that people *lived*? I
thought of a scene in Dr. Zhivago; he had just said goodbye to his lover
Lara and headed back through the forest to his wife. The trees made
a long column on either side. He was fraught with indecision. Lara?
Wife? Lara? His horse, with no guidance from him, slowed, walked, finally stopped. But Zhivago's fate was determined by history. At that
moment, the Red Army came galloping out of the woods. A soldier
grabbed his horse's reins and swept him away. I wanted to be subsumed in that same awful way. To be moved by forces larger than myself, to be made blameless.

Russia saved me from my depression. Another exotic spectacle, en-
ticingly scary in the last days of Brezhnev. In September I embarked
on the first of nine trips there. In Russia I was charmed by the famous
"Russian soul," galvanized by a world in which people had to close a
door to tell a joke, in which punishment was so swift and irrational,
so like my family.

Kim stood barefoot, in cutoffs, spraying poison on his thriving vegetable garden. No organics for him; that was just silliness. Everyone
overreacting. He'd called or I called because I was in Vermont again,
visiting my mother; Kim must have figured enough time had gone by
for us to try again, at least to be friends. I wandered the rooms my
mother had decorated for him, as restless as the long-legged, weaving
wolves at the zoo in Colorado where Kim's mother snapped a picture
of us so many years ago. Kim led me upstairs to his bedroom, bourbon glass in hand. I hated that whiskey smell; it was more than on his
breath. It emanated from his pores now.

"Will you make love with me?" he asked.

"I don't want to," I said.

"Well can't you just lie there anyway?"

I stared. His eyes looked crazed, foreign and frighteningly fixed. A blue that received no light, reflective eyes boiled hard in their whites.

"No," I said. "I can't believe you want me to." We'd sunk to some new low if he could want to have sex with my rigid, resistant body. It wasn't me he wanted. It was the *idea* of me he needed to fuck now. I couldn't do this anymore.

I heard from my mother, who assiduously kept up with Kim, that he'd abruptly quit working the study skills business after nine years and left town. He was living at his parents' house, working as the managing editor of Garrett's magazine. Garrett had gotten it off the ground, though it wasn't the political and social commentary slick he'd hoped for; rather, he'd settled for a "lifestyle" magazine devoted to the new wealth that followed Denver's boom.

Kim and I spoke once on the phone. "Why don't you get your own place?" I asked. "You could move to Boulder or Denver."

"No time."

"What do you mean no time?"

"There's a lot of work to be done on the magazine and I have to do it."

"It's not all up to you."

"Yes it is," he insisted peevishly. Kim, at twenty, believed he had to take care of his parents. Now he thought he had to run the magazine by himself. In a gentler tone, Kim added, "You know, I always watch the weather channel to see what kind of weather you're having."

I went to the northern office of the educational firm that had em-
ployed Kim to talk to Syd Greene, who was running it now. Syd and
Kim had worked together. The business is located in an ordinary two-
story white house on a corner a block or two back from the strip development leading into a college town. I expected something more
grand, remembering Henry Huntley's luxurious office in Vermont. Upstairs, across from Syd's office, I noted a room with a double bed made
up, an oddity for an office. *Did Syd sleep there?* I wondered. Syd, too,
was unprepossessing. A small, balding man who didn't meet my eyes
came to the door. He wore a fanny pack in front and could have been
someone's tired Jewish uncle. As our talk went on, I couldn't help
wondering about his life. For years he had spent six months teaching, six months abroad. Kim had said that Syd wrote plays. What had

kept him from a more settled existence? Did he have one now? He looked deeply sad.

He said, "I can't tell you much. I saw Kim infrequently for years. We were both teaching; we barely intersected." But as we talked, a picture of Kim in the office took shape. Syd described a more on-the-wagon/off-the-wagon life than I had imagined. "In 1981 or so," Syd said, "Kim took over the northern office when Henry moved down south. But it eventually became clear that the accounts were all messed up, that it was all chaos, that Kim's drinking made him incompetent and they had to tell him to go get himself cleaned up, dried out, and then he could come back. Instead of drying out, Kim moved to Denver to work at a magazine."

A piece of the picture fell in place: Kim's sudden move to Denver after refusing Garrett's offer to work on the magazine. I felt embarrassed and hurt for him that he'd had to be removed, told to clean himself up. Taking the job with Garrett was as much a flight from failure as it was a movement toward a new challenge.

"But he came back to work for you after a few years," I said, "and he must have still been drinking. Why did you and Henry keep him on for so long? Why did you carry him?" I asked.

"Kim was enormously valuable. You don't just throw people away. He helped to build up the business. He got all those accounts in the Midwest, Texas, all across the center of the country between here and Colorado. And he alone had that information."

Was it self interest, then? They kept him on because he had the western account information?

Syd continued. "It's exciting to help build up a business. And the days when we were designing the writing program, which really never went very far, because English departments were so threatened by it, those were exciting times too. It was a part of my life shared with Kim and now Kim is gone. Kim did so much in terms of program development and design. He was a workaholic and he was a wonderful teacher. He'd set himself a schedule of teaching eight periods a day, so he could have eight small classes instead of four big ones. That's what I had to take over when Kim had to be removed from a course at Brown University for showing up drunk."

"That's when he was finally fired?" I asked. Henry Huntley had mentioned to me on the phone that after the Brown incident Kim had hung around the office for a few weeks, trying to work for free, then disappeared.

"He *wasn't* fired," Syd insisted. "He was told to clean himself up. After the loss of Brown, after his mother's death, Kim was in Nebraska somewhere and he called very apologetic, and said how sorry he was for all the trouble he'd caused the last two years, and wanted to send back his salary. I told him we just wanted him to get himself cleaned up and be productive again."

"Was he sober when he called?" I asked.

"He seemed sober."

That call, that apology, intrigues and torments me: Kim alone in that hotel room somewhere in Nebraska, faced with his life. So there was at least one moment in which Kim acknowledged, admitted the damages his drinking had wrought. And Kim, when sober, was still concerned with being a moral man. He wanted to make restitution.

Syd added, "He broke his ankle before the episode at Brown, refused to go to a doctor, limped around for six months. He broke his ankle playing basketball. He used to do that, play games of basketball, use gym facilities."

I wondered if that was, in fact, how he'd broken his ankle or if that's just what he told Syd. I wanted to believe in a Kim healthy enough to still shoot baskets, so near the end, but I feared he had hurt himself while drunk. He probably refused to go to doctors because they'd notice his alcoholism. "Do you know how else he spent his time outside of work?" I ventured.

Syd shook his head. "He was impossible socially. I invited him to come for dinner for twenty years, and he never came. He never talked about his personal life, except to mention his brother, whom he didn't like very much, or his mother, whom he did. When he started teaching again, he spent two and a half months a year working his way back to Colorado every summer, and no one knows what he did, how he lived. He went to schools and made presentations. He took it upon himself to make a presentation at the Air Force Academy in Colorado, and he was so drunk he could barely speak. We found out six months later when we got a call.

"When he was drinking his mind slowed down and it was terribly painful to watch. He could only say one word at a time, and sometimes not even that, so he spoke almost entirely through these hand gestures." Syd raised his hands and stared at them, fingers splayed and tense; he turned them, studied them. "You could see him struggling to say something but he couldn't get it out."

"Aphasic," I said. "Like a stroke victim."

"Yes. He had a psychotic episode. He came to work one day sure that everything in his world had been changed overnight. Someone had come in and switched all the furniture in his motel room. His whole world had been replaced. This went on for about a week and a half, and we called his mother and brother, and they came and committed him to the hospital. The problem was he would go cold turkey. He couldn't accept any help, couldn't go along with AA. There was a string of car accidents. Every nine months or so another."

"Did he still write? He was always working on this book," I said.

"That stopped a long time ago. I'd offer him books—we used to talk about books we read, but all that was lost. I thought he'd be interested in Mirsky's book on Artificial Intelligence because it was connected to what we were trying to do with breaking down learning into components—and he'd take them, and eventually send them back with no comment. I don't know if he read them or not. He only wanted to talk about teaching strategies. He was always very pleasant, very meticulous, very diligent."

"He used to write in such a tiny print," I said.

"He kept that cramped little handwriting to the end. He'd sit there writing, writing, although it said nothing."

"Do you miss him?" I asked.

"Yes, I suppose I do."

"Is his death also a relief?"

Syd shook his head. "No."

Driving home, I kept thinking of Kim at a motel, waking up disoriented to find that someone, somehow had removed the furniture and all his belongings, had switched them. It seems too perfect a metaphor for what really happened—his whole life got replaced by that of a drunk.

The woman who had worked with Kim when he ran the Vermont office said, "He was devastated when you two broke up. He always mentioned you. Some people just can't deal. My new boss is so nice and laid back he reminds me of Kim. See, Kim always comes to mind."

1984–1988

Morrissey, June 4, 1984

OK. *So you finally found a way to make me write . . . use Latin.*

Accuse me of quid pro quo *(that's probably true); accuse me of* mutatis mutandis *(that's inevitable); but never, never accuse me of* non sequitur.

I have faced the tribunal before on this charge. The transcript follows:

Tribunal: Do you depend on this madness for your livelihood?

Me: Yes.

Tribunal: Does this madness require infinite work?

Me: Yes.

Tribunal: Who else will do this work?

Me: No one.
Tribunal: Then who must.
Me: Me.
Case closed.

In fact, I will take time off this summer.
I'd like to spend some of it with you. Mexico, the World's Fair, San Francisco—you tell me. I did not feel the pressure cooking, and the only clicking I know has to do with crickets. (Actually, they scrape, and at least we didn't do that this time.) Laurie, I think you're still looking for magic. I am many things, but one of the things I'm not is magic. Let me know your plans. I look forward to seeing you again.
> Love,
> Kim

As it worked out, I didn't see Kim; we didn't go to Mexico or San Francisco. I continued to travel to Russia. In my friends' Leningrad apartment we drank tea after an evening out. Sergei examined a wooden box he was carving. Lyuda set out her watercolors and began a portrait of me. The children slept in the bedroom. Sergei took up a tiny chisel and began to slide it gently, steadily with the grain. "It's better at home," he said.

"It is," I replied. For the first time, I thought, *There's something here I might want.* Not continual excitement, but this camaraderie, this peace. What Kim had offered long ago, only now it was too late.

My mother kept up with Kim's mother and relayed news. Kim's father had died and shy Gloria was a realtor now. With my condolence letter I sent Gloria a picture I'd taken of John, standing on the tailgate of his truck, grinning, a straw sombrero on his head. I didn't hear from her (though for many years she'd sent me cards with religious themes), which I accepted as a comment on my treatment of her son. Or, perhaps, she was too overwhelmed by grief and the need to make a living. Then came the news that Kim, after three years, had left the Denver magazine as abruptly as he'd left the East; he was back with Huntley again, living in motels. He didn't want to run the business, merely teach. I received a letter.

May 11, 1986

Hi Laurie,

Tonight I'm in New Orleans. (I stopped at home along the way to start the garden, and in a day or two I'll be back to pick the weeds. Then I intend to go fishing. This promises to be my best summer in years.)

I'll be teaching at Wesleyan next fall. Will you be around? You said you were tired of Russia (forget Chernobyl—it's been obscured by hype); where else would you like to go? Will you be going this fall? If not, I'd like to see you. Let me know. Otherwise, I threaten to call.

     Kim

P.S. I'd also like to read your book, but I won't push it. You get angry when I do.

May 18, 1986

Laurie,

Strange.

A week ago I wrote to you for the first time in several years. The proximate cause was my presence in New Orleans, where a portion of the city reminded me of New York. This, in turn, reminded me of you. In passing (to protect myself) I mentioned again my interest in reading your book. Now I hear it's going to be published, and once it's in the public domain, my curiosity cannot be denied. Need I tell you how happy I am . . . or need I tell you for whom?

     Kim

I agreed to meet Kim because I'd heard, through my mother again, that he'd gone into a detox. He had told his mother, "I can't stop drinking." I don't suppose that Gloria offered this information; my mother must have drawn it out. Kim had never admitted he had a problem before; I wondered how deep this change went. It wasn't a rehab, just a two-day stint in a hospital where they'd given him antibuse, a chemical that makes you sick if you drink. I had no fantasies of a renewed romance but I wanted to see this sober Kim. And, though it shames me to admit it, I had another motive. Kim was the only witness to my adolescence outside of my family. I wanted to know what he'd seen.

I was still living in a maid's room in New York, traveling back and forth to Russia as a tour guide and, when I was home, caretaking a wealthy friend's epileptic, retarded, and perhaps schizophrenic uncle. Uncle Donny was harmless enough, even if he occasionally lapsed into mild hallucinations. I drove Donny from Manhattan to the family's Connecticut country house in their Volvo station wagon each weekend. Donny always brought along his cat in one travel case and a stack of porno in the other. It was a cushy if slightly creepy job; I had only to drive, buy groceries, and cook. The phenobarbital Donny took to control seizures made him sleep until noon. The rest of the time he liked to sort screws and nails in his workshop and make calls to a prostitute he insisted was his girlfriend. I was paid well, got out of the city, and had plenty of time to write.

I left Donny to one of his projects that Saturday and drove into Westport to a bookstore-café. I went early. I needed time to compose myself; I wanted to be seated, protected somehow, when Kim came in. Though we'd written and spoken a few times, I hadn't seen Kim since that day in his bedroom when he wanted me to "just lie there."

I ordered coffee and watched the prosperous, patrician Westport folk sip their cappuccinos, read their New York Times, nibble their pastries. I tried to concentrate on a newspaper but my eyes kept skidding off the page. The colorful spines of stacked books shone from the shelves; big coffee table tomes and glossy calendars decorated display tables. I glanced at the wall clock. Five minutes more.

Kim loomed over the table, as tall and straight as ever. His hair had grayed some; it was short and neatly trimmed. He looked healthy but subdued.

"Laurie," he said.

"Hi, Kim."

It hurt to watch his eyes drink me in, memorizing me, feeding his cells something as necessary to their altered function as the booze he—perhaps—had given up.

"You're still a very attractive woman," Kim said.

I shrugged. I was thirty-three and my black hair had silver threads. New York had taught me to consider myself no prize. After coffee we sat on the cold sand of the Westport public beach, squinting into weak spring sun. Down the strand a man threw a ball repeatedly for his black lab. The panting, drooling dog's enthusiasm seemed misplaced. The greenish water lay unruffled by waves; the coarse sand had been carted in. Not like the sugary dunes of the Cape Cod beach where, when I was seventeen, Kim and I made love, the scent of crabs and seaweed in my nostrils, the sun reddening my closed eyelids, the grains of sand pushing inside me with each thrust.

I said, "I heard you did a detox."

"I'm an alcoholic," Kim said softly. "Neither of my parents drank, but both my grandfathers were alcoholics. They say it can skip a generation."

I sighed. It was the first time he'd ever admitted it to me. I wondered how the grandfathers' alcoholism had shaped his parents' lives, and therefore his. I remembered the unopened bottle of dark purple Mogen David wine, a permanent fixture, in the Janiks' refrigerator. When did they ever bother to crack the cap? A syrupy drop on New Year's Eve? An otherwise dry house.

"Are you going to AA meetings?" I asked. "You know, getting continuing help?"

Kim shook his head. "You know how I feel about the God stuff, Laurie."

"Some people find AA helpful even without the higher power. I've been going to meetings, not AA, but another twelve-step program."

Kim listened carefully.

"I've been trying to figure out stuff." I pinched up a handful of gravelly sand, released it. "I was wondering, when I was a teenager, did you ever notice my father treating me sexually? You know, saying inappropriate things?"

"Yes, I did," Kim said softly.

Tears came to my eyes. "You really did?" I didn't think to ask him what he'd seen, I was so overwhelmed with vindication.

"Yes."

"My sister and brother don't believe me. They say I'm being dramatic, making up things."

Kim shook his head. "I didn't know what to do, Laurie."

Grateful, I leaned forward to touch his arm and stiffened—could that be bourbon on his breath?

Kim followed me back to Uncle Donny's house to play with my first computer. I'd set it up in the master bedroom. An enormous bed and the erotic painting above it made me nervous with Kim there, but he sat down at the computer excitedly. He wanted to show me some tricks. When we huddled together over the keyboard I was sure I smelled booze on his breath. He was lying. Not lying, but allowing me, by omission, to believe he'd stopped drinking.

Kim stood up from the computer. "I always read the *New York Times Book Review* looking for a review of your work," he said.

"There's never been anything to see."

"But now there will be. I guess I can wait until it comes out, but I'd really like to read your Alaska book in manuscript. Could I?"

Although he'd put hours into discussing the early draft with me, I didn't want him to read it. I knew it would hurt him to see how little he'd figured in that part of my life, how large other men had loomed, even in fiction. Reluctantly I turned over the gray cardboard box that held the pages. (It came back a week later with only the words "it's good" printed in Kim's tiny, cramped hand. For once he'd been unwilling to discuss my work.)

Downstairs, a crash. Donny had dropped something in his workshop.

"I guess I better be going," Kim said.

He didn't try to linger, to drag out his visit. I thought he might be eager to get back to whatever room he had rented, to the bottle I was sure he had stashed. To the one thing, now, that drew him more than I did.

A train station in Rome. My arm hung out the window and Graziano, on the platform, held my fingers, stared intently into my eyes. "I like, I like to touch you, I like you to touch me, I like to make certain movements inside you . . ." But the train was late taking off and my arm got tired. I ran out of things to say and the guy suspended out the next window was blowing cigarette smoke in my eyes. It was ludicrous. I'd met narrow-hipped Graziano in the Tarot pizzeria. I was sitting alone at a table under a painting of "The Devil" from the tarot deck—a chained naked man and woman. Graziano asked to sit down. I gestured at the picture and said, "The devil, my old friend." My first mistake. We went to a bar in which the drink menu read "school driver" for "screwdriver," and then to his apartment. Now, when the train finally chugged slowly off, Graziano followed me with mournful eyes. Perhaps he was acting too, playing out his role. I wondered how long before I could decently turn my head and quit waving. I was too old for this. There wasn't adventure in it anymore. It was just stupid.

After seven years of living in New York City I moved with friends to the country for the summer. My therapist allowed me to have a session at her summerhouse, a converted barn in upstate New York. We sat on lawn chairs in her green yard while her lesbian lover took their child for a walk along a stony brook that bordered their property. I was touched that Beth would interrupt her vacation time to help me cope with my depression. Seven years had passed since I first came to her door. I had never once been able to meet her eyes. Outside of her office I had a straightforward gaze; I'd even been charged with staring. (My mother used to accuse me of giving men a "come hither look.") Yet I couldn't glance up when I talked to Beth. On some cellular level I sensed that to acknowledge the existence of someone who cared for me would be to destroy myself. This time I peered into the long, plain freckled face of this woman who had made room for me in her summer day. In her even, blue-eyed gaze I felt a direct current of simple concern. A thousand glass fragments ground inside my chest. I was falling, crumbling, disintegrating—dizzy and gasping. Quickly I looked away again. But it was too late to batten down. I'd let someone in.

My mother reported from time to time that she invited Kim to dinner when he was in Vermont, but after she told him about my marriage, he never called her back, never answered her letters; she never saw him again. When I thought of Kim I chased him from my mind, chased away our history and all the regret, sorrow, and resignation that went with it. Occasionally I had to contend with the darkness, the voice that told me, when I was driving alone, to jerk the steering wheel, to veer into a stone wall, but I knew that no one else could save me. Still, in moments of fear or humiliation, I couldn't help silently shaping Kim's name.

I learned about Kim's death by a fluke, and didn't learn much. On a trip
to Colorado my mother had tried to look up Gloria and found no Janik listing. She called her former landlord, Kim's employer. All he knew
was that Kim had died alone in a wilderness somewhere out west.

Frantic for information, I sat in my University of New Mexico office with the door closed, dialing newspapers and morgues. I came up
empty. I tried the Pittsford, Colorado, Police Department in hopes
that Matt still worked there. They wouldn't give me his unlisted phone
number, but they gave him my number in New Mexico, and Matt called
me promptly. "I tried to contact you when it happened," Matt said,
"but I didn't know how to find you."

I shut my eyes at the sound of his Colorado accent, so familiar after all the years, so like Kim's. "Was it suicide?" I asked. "Henry Huntley thought it was."

"No, it wasn't suicide. Kim was always driving around with his fishing equipment in his car, camping by lakes and streams. He said he was going to build a cabin in Montana or someplace. He was a lost, sad, lonely man, Laurie. But he didn't mean to kill himself."

I think now of Ted Kaczynski, the Unabomber, with his cabin in Montana, another lost academic, though his rage had turned outward rather than inward. Could Kim have been happy in a cabin in some wilderness? Tom, an ardent fisherman, believes that despite Kim's miseries, he could have retained joy in fishing, in the landscape, until the end.

Matt relayed an ugly history of Kim's car crashes and hospitals, half-gallon vodka bottles mixed with Gatorade, the d.t.'s, and an attack on his mother with a screwdriver. "I watched my brother, an intelligent man, turn into a stumbling drunk. He lived in these dive motels, Laurie. I picked him up one time after one of his incidents and drove him back west. I had to keep the truck window open. He stunk like a Bowery bum."

I flinched. Surely Kim hadn't gone that far downhill.

"I was always expecting to hear that Kim had killed someone in a car crash," Matt said. "I told him," Matt's voice rose angrily as if he were addressing Kim, "'You do that, and I'll personally kill you!' Laurie, I was relieved when I got the call."

Somewhere along the line Matt and Kim had reversed roles. First it was Kim, then Matt, worrying about the other's failings.

Matt continued, "I told him one time, 'Maybe if you would've quit drinking Laurie wouldn't have left you.' He got upset so I didn't push it."

I bit my lip. How little Matt knew of our history. It was easy to remain silent, to let Matt think that I had left Kim because of booze. "Did he ever get married?" I asked. "Did he have kids? I hoped he'd made some kind of life."

"His only relationship was the bottle." In a softer tone Matt said, "I remember when you came out that first time. You two sure seemed stuck on each other. I've got a picture of the two of you back then. It was in Kim's car when he died. I keep it on my mantel."

"Could I see the picture sometime?" I asked.

"It belongs to you."

"And how have you been, Matt?"

"Oh, none the worse for wear. I don't drink because of Kim."

Matt provided the facts but no explanations. When I found Garrett's listing in Denver, I thought that he might not know who I was. It had been more than twenty years since I'd waited outside his office while he and Kim conferred. He said, "Yes, I remember you. You were very attractive." Garrett had seen Kim a few weeks before he died. "I called him and he met me for dinner. I wanted help with a new magazine I was starting. He was sitting in the lounge reading a *Scientific American* when I arrived."

Reading *Scientific American*? So Kim was still curious, still thinking weeks before he died. I grasped onto the information, a counter to Matt's vision of him as a Bowery bum. "He wasn't . . . seedy?" I asked.

"No, he was clean, dressed well, but I was stunned he looked so old. He was so pale he looked like he'd been taken directly from the morgue. His hair was completely white. He seemed genuinely happy to see me, like a reunion. We talked for a while about what he was reading—about frogs. How they'd been around for millions of years and now they were dying and mutating. He showed me some pictures. They were green and yellow, you know, frogs.

"When he reached for a glass his hands shook. He made very tentative movements."

Garrett paused. "It's hard to talk about Kim . . . Going to the table I wanted to take his arm to help him. He seemed like he was on something, like he wasn't with it. I knew there was diminished capacity, as diminished as he was before, this was ten years later. He looked pallid, sickly, withdrawn. My expectations were dashed. Purely selfishly, I knew I wouldn't get help and I wanted help. He promised he'd write a few pages for me but he never sent them."

I plagued everyone who'd known Kim with questions. Had they seen this coming? Were there clues? What did they remember about him?

My mother said, "There was a particular quality to Kim's voice that I liked. Musical. He was adorable. I always saw him as a good-natured, even guy, but I also saw he had some compulsive habits. He had a plan and method for doing dishes—he'd correct you if you did it wrong. He came down to the Cape at Thanksgiving. You two had an argument. I saw him outside sitting on the step. I remember feeling angry at you for treating him that way. I was trying to throw off the anger. I brought it up to you. You got mad. You said, 'You don't know what he did to me.'

"He was so proud of that place in Putney. He was overjoyed with that house. Then he left so suddenly. The furniture went into storage in Brattleboro. He said he'd come back for it. He paid for the furniture storage for twelve years. It wasn't worth it. I thought it was part of his not being able to let go of the dream of you being in his life. You owned land here."

My father said: "I thought he had a very bright future ahead of him. His first mistake was giving up ROTC."

My brother, Charlie, a computer company executive, reminisced about meeting Kim when he was fourteen. "I thought Kim was the coolest guy around. He was hip, at Harvard, older, and exceptionally nice, so nice. He talked to me, he listened to me. I was mixed up, doing drugs. He was a maturing influence on me. He took a very genuine interest in me apart from you. He drove me to Worcester to get parts for a go-cart I was building. He took me along with you to see *I Am Curious Yellow*.

"I wasn't aware of problems between you. The three of us went camping once in Colorado, in the Maroon Bells. I didn't have the right boots; the altitude bothered me. Kim carried my tent, my heavy stuff. Remember, we named this squirrel Kowalski? You two were sharing an apartment in Boulder. You seemed happy, very domestic."

Strange that my perceptive little brother had noticed no problems. Perhaps there were peaceful stretches of time long after the Harvard days that I've forgotten in light of the many fights, the break-ups, my defections. An alternate explanation for why we kept returning to each other.

"I loved Kim immensely," Charlie said. "He never asked anything of me. He was always giving. He was a true big brother. I was too young to understand or reciprocate. His helpfulness buffered the world for me."

"That's how he was with everybody," I said. "At least until the booze took over. He thought he had to take care of his parents, that they couldn't cope."

"I imagine his role with his parents was like a hearing child with deaf parents," Charlie said. "The last time I saw him he came to our apartment in Northampton to give us a wedding gift, a boxed set of Chopin albums. He wouldn't come in. I feel bad that I didn't do anything to help him. He's probably the person who has been kindest to me in my entire life."

Months, a year passed and still I had dreams:

Winter '97

I was in a store. I opened a drawer in a bureau and found it full of my tiny anorexia clothes from high school. I was sifting through them. Then the dream shifted and I received a call from Kim. He told me he was going to kill himself. He just wanted me to know. Wait, I said, Wait. But our connection was broken. I frantically tried to locate him through directory assistance but I couldn't get through.

Winter '97

I dreamed of searching for information about Kim in Cambridge. Went to Quincy House, found the British math tutor who had lived next door to Kim was still there. She would say only that they were worried about Kim back then. How could they have been worried about him then? Outside, I got caught in a narrow side street. Someone was dumping an enormous load of bricks from a truck and I had to try to protect myself by pressing against the building. Then I was in a glass restaurant with a view of the ocean, and I was running from room to room. Once again something large and dangerous fell over me. I had to dive down, down, down into the water. I didn't know if it was safe to come up yet, but I was running out of air. So I surfaced.

Waiting for the airport limo to take me to Bradley International en route to Colorado, I joked to Tom, "Kim and I had a lot in common. We were both obsessed with me."

I picked up my rental car at the Denver airport and drove straight to Morrissey, to the cemetery. Dusk was coming on, midsummer dusk, a chill in the high, dry Colorado air. In purpling twilight I found Gloria and John's single gravestone, pinkish granite inscribed with a flowery flourish and the words: "Sorrow is not forever . . . love is." John's date of birth and death were carved on it, and Gloria's name and birth date, but there was no death date for her, as though, once she died, the family lost its definition and, with it, the ability to complete rituals.

Matt had told me on the phone that Kim's ashes were buried beside their parents' grave, but there was no marker, just a broken plastic flowerpot spilling potting soil, a few dried stalks that might not even have been for him. Didn't anyone think he was worthy of a gravestone?

I slept that night in a dumpy motel in Pittsford, one town south of Morrissey, the sort of place Kim would have stayed in. I did it to save money and, perhaps, to try on his life. The reception clerk sat behind a Plexiglas partition and slid my key under a two-inch opening. A tattoo parlor was situated next door. The hall carpet was torn, the clientele sleazy. I was fearful because the lock on my room was a simple button job, no dead bolt, let alone the fancy keyless kind you open with a card. I called home and spoke to Tom and my little daughter.

"Why do you have to be away, Mommy?" Becky wanted to know. I couldn't shape an answer that she, at four, would understand. I slept with pepper spray by my pillow.

In the morning I drove around Morrissey, willing myself to recognize places, but the town had gentrified. The Janiks' old house, beige now, looked as neat and orderly as ever. It wasn't just the gentrification that had changed the town. The Morrissey of twenty-five years ago would no longer strike me as impoverished as it had then. Since my first shocked visit, I had lived in so many cabins and shacks and maids' rooms and one-room walkups, had scrounged for money and gone without so often, that now it appeared to me merely modest.

However, much of Morrissey was no longer modest. In a Main Street café adorned with antiques, I drank a latte. A group of young mothers, whose kids were licking cones at a table, talked loudly: "We wanted to stretch to buy a five-hundred-thousand-dollar home. You make the payments, and you have a lovely home. Now, some people can't stretch, like my sister. She's a teacher and she's never going to make more than cost of living increases . . . Adam, put that card back. Someone else will want to buy it and they'll want it fresh."

"Yeah," another mom chimed in, "they won't want sticky ice cream hands all over it."

On the wall near the door hung a realtor's listing. In Morrissey, in 1997, only an ugly raised ranch cost less than $200,000, and not by much.

I moved on to Boulder, a shimmering city of small parks and greenswards nestled up against the sandstone slabs of the front range. There was no sign of the chaos of the early seventies. The town was radiant with health, the foothills speckled with joggers and spandexed bikers leaning over handlebars, no more violent STP families and park squatters.

Gone was the little peaked house on the hill where I snuck through Kim's window at night. It had been replaced by a tall stucco apartment building.

I retreated to the city library. Guiltily I sought out my own book titles, perhaps to confirm my existence in a town in which the geography of my past had disappeared. In the periodical room, feeling ghoulish, I dug up articles about my friend Michael Dorris, who had committed suicide in April, seeking explanations for my dead. The magazines told me nothing I wanted to know, gossip and speculation and dirt. What I searched for in those slick and glossy pages was unanswerable.

In three years, three of my friends had destroyed themselves. Kim, Michael, and back in Vermont, my friend Rita—whose teenage son had shot himself at home five years earlier. Rita drove into the woods, stuck a hose into her tailpipe, and died listening to gospel music. She left her denim jacket in my closet with a recipe for chocolate chip cookies in the breast pocket, and unfilled plans for us to go horseback riding together that week.

In the absence of our visible history, mine and Kim's, I was left juggling these self-destructions. And wondering how I escaped. If you compared the two of us in those years when I was shaking on that Arizona highway, or fishing alone out of an open skiff in Alaskan winter, or seeing double as I drove drunk on the winding Vermont roads at night, or lying on the edge of a roof in New York contemplating rolling off, you would think that I was the one at greater risk, not he.

Maybe I was tougher than Kim was. The shrieking, the night trip to the emergency ward, the car chasing us down the driveway, that which had given me demons and walled me off had also made me harder to defeat. Kim's gentleness and his self-deceit doomed him. Maybe I survived because I had Kim.

Beside the Boulder library ran a creek with cottonwoods, golden in the afternoon light. I sat on a bench here twenty-five years ago reading Brautigan's *In Watermelon Sugar* as though he—another suicide—might tell me how to live.

Though I drove back and forth on the two-lane county road, I couldn't find the turnoff to the old tar-paper ranch house where I had lived with Chris and his housemates. I tried to orient myself by the white gypsum hills that I'd once stared at while the sagebrush wavered and whispered my name. But the hills I recalled as bare geometries, etched with the lines of erosion, were covered now in trees. Did I remember them as more stark because I hadn't yet lived six years in parched New Mexico, or had they filled in during the last twenty-five years? (It was only when I was back home and looking at a photo I'd taken from the ranch in 1971 that I realized the white hills still existed. I'd been too close, this time, to see them above the tree line.)

The uplands of endless cedar and sage and cracked dry earth are now chopped into a housing development with streets named for game birds: Pintail and Grouse. Farther along the road, past where the turnoff to the old ranch should have been, lay fields with horses, cattle; white frame bungalows stood under tall shade trees, bikes and toys in their yards. I never knew that this orderly world existed so close to the eerie sagelands, the farmer's dump of broken blue glass and dented cans and a twisted cowboy boot where I had whiled away my shaky days. But they must have been here then; these houses looked old, established.

The fields were too green, too grassy. I had lived here in hunting season, the fields beige with dead grass and the toppled bodies of deer. Now they held huge bread loaf–shaped hay mounds.

Back in Eagle I went into a saloon and did something I never do: I ordered a drink at 10:50 in the morning, once again trying on Kim's life. The waitress, in hot pink spandex shorts and long bleached hair, with a face that had been around the block, brought me a too strong rum and Diet Coke. The place was populated by women. I expected male drinkers, like the VFW in Brattleboro where I once took my driver's test at nine in the morning and saw, through a doorway, men hunched along the bar. I sipped my drink and read the local rag, marveling at the huge, inflated real estate prices. Now there were golf courses on the mesas, and Avon, just a stretch of mobile homes back then, was packed with condos, cheaply constructed, overpriced ski homes. People worked "down valley," the waitress said, in Vail or the other ski areas that had cropped up between Vail and Eagle. This land that had once struck me as unutterably desolate, exotic, and ominous was merely badly used.

In Minturn, I couldn't find our old log shack in a trailer park. Instead there were antiques and curios and restaurants and galleries and import houses and a French bakery in which people actually spoke French. It was still a cute little false-fronted railroad town, too narrow a canyon to build the big condos. Perhaps it was also saved by its lack of big peak views—a river valley cut between sage hills, Russian olives blowing their gray-green leaves. Boys trimmed geraniums and petunias in flower boxes. It looked wrong to me, as if the main road into town had been moved, the railroad bar gone. Could my memory be that inaccurate to shift the landscape?

I felt Kim's absence more in Minturn than in Morrissey at his unmarked grave. I looked into the clear run of the Eagle River, its beige and brown rocks, a river from which Kim pulled many a trout. I saw the shadow of Kim crouched in the creekside boulders so as not to scare away the fish, his wet tennis shoes, his bare golden legs, the fluorescent pinky orange of the salmon eggs he sometimes used for bait. Kim across a river, and still life flows through me, my heart pumps.

It's the inexorability of time I see—the wiping away of our history, of his existence. I write to stop time, to hold water flowing through my fingers.

This place scares me—the abyss—gussied up with Colorado summer sunshine, hammer blows, the boys across the street in the midst of their own invented lives—ski bums? New Jersey escapees? One yawns, lifts a bucket of tools. You don't know, I think, this is a blink under the sun's indifferent furnace, and then the glittering distance of a night sky awaits you.

I found Matt's house in Erie, nine miles north of Morrissey. To get there I crossed prairie land, huge flat fields squared and plowed and planted, interrupted by housing development clusters. Thunderheads hung over the wall of Rockies, a vertical boundary to the west. When I pulled into Matt's yard he was working his quarter horse Zero in a ring. He dismounted and put his horse away, unzipped his chaps. Matt looked good, very tan, only a bit wrinkled around the eyes. His blue eyes with black dotted pupils were beautiful. He wasn't chunky as he'd been, just had a little gut, nothing remarkable for a man his—our— age. He struck me as tall now, though I remembered him as short— in comparison to Kim, I suppose.

Though a nurse, Matt's younger girlfriend, Becky, resembled a cow- girl with her strong cheekbones, fluffy layered hair, very tight jeans over a round butt, cinched small waist. There was lots of teasing and laughing between them, though it had an edge: Matt chucked peb- bles at her as a joke.

By the barn, an Akita pulled at his chain. Matt's yard, landscaped with pine bark chips and volcanic rocks and concrete borders, was strikingly neat. The barnyard looked as though it were swept daily. While we sat drinking iced tea on his patio, Matt got up to spray a wasp with insecticide. I could taste the poison on my tongue.

Matt was glad to see me, but probably puzzled by my trip here, my persistent questions about Kim's last years. "You shouldn't blame yourself," Matt said. "No matter what, if you had taken him back, he couldn't have given up the bottle. His whole life was arranged around his drinking. He drove at night to avoid cops. There were warrants out for his arrest in Colorado and other states."

I couldn't bring myself to say that it was more complicated than that. I couldn't sit here in Matt's perfectly ordered yard and tell him anything of the years of my disordered behavior and the ways in which Kim suffered for it.

When I asked about Kim's youth, Matt replied, "I can't say I real- ly knew Kim. I hung out with the ranch kids; Kim was a bookworm. A very quiet kid."

Again we went over the details of Kim's terrible death. "Do you think he knew he was dying?" I asked. The thought of him lying there, too weak to move, knowing that he'd reached the end, was appalling.

"I don't think so. He just knew he didn't feel well."

I wondered if Matt were trying to protect me. Earlier he'd called it a "violent death." Had he meant dehydration and hypothermia are violent?

Matt retrieved the promised photograph when I asked. I studied the faded snapshot. With the pipe in his mouth, his startled expression, Kim's features were hard to discern. I recognized myself, though, that camera-wise smirk.

Garrett's house, on an upscale Denver street, was low, long, expensive. Two Jaguars sat side by side in Garrett's garage, both his. Garrett had warned me on the phone that due to a health condition he'd lost all his body hair. Still, I was stunned by his shiny dome, his lack of eyebrows and lashes, the pallor above his natty suit.

I wondered if I were a disappointment to Garrett. Had he expected, however improbably, that I would be that same "attractive" nineteen-year-old who had waited for Kim outside his Denver office instead of a woman in her forties, haunted and obsessed? Perhaps I, being dropped into my past after twenty-five years, half expected that of myself.

He relayed his history with Kim: "I called Kim in '81 and asked him to come on board the magazine. Kim thought about it and called back and said no, he wasn't right for the job, but then in '83 he called me and asked if he could work for me."

"That was after he messed up the office in Vermont and was told to clean up," I said. "You probably didn't know that."

"No, but I was aware from day one that he had a drinking problem."

"Then why did you tolerate him?"

"Because he tolerated me. No other person I worked with showed me as much tolerance and kindness as Kim did.

"In the mornings he did great writing. By the afternoons he stumbled. One Saturday morning I was there, Kim was there, not a regular workday, and he was drinking, I smelled it, and I said, 'Kim, what are we going to do about this drinking habit you've got that needs addressing?' Kim said, 'I'm not drinking.' The second time I brought it up he said, 'Do I do my job well enough to earn my pay?'

"He did; I got my money's worth. Kim could edit a manuscript while he was heavily under the influence better than most people I hired who were sober. He would do ninety-nine tasks perfectly and screw up one. He had a marvelous rapport with the editorial staff. Kim was the executive editor, the man of last resort. He made the final cuts and additions. He was responsible for polish editing, proofreading. He loved it. The layout, design, the editing. He had a good sense for captions; he was a teacher, an instructor. When he changed something of a writer's, he explained why. People appreciated his help. He was extremely kind, but he was also aloof. He had an austerity. People didn't go into his office and joke with him. There was a distance. You could get close professionally but not personally. He wouldn't even come to the office Christmas luncheon.

"Another editor used to cover for him. She'd make meetings with writers, the printer, in the mornings, because she knew by afternoon Kim would be too far gone."

I remembered Kim's insistence to me that his work was endless and he had to do everything; nobody else could do it—when half of the time the staff was covering for him. The combination of ability and self-deception pained me. I remember too, his enthusiasm—issues he showed me, an article he'd written on Malcolm Forbes's hot air balloons, a piece on stained-glass windows in some cathedral.

"He got going on this project, creating a database of all the advertisers. It took enormous amounts of time—he'd type away, mostly afternoons when he was inebriated, but he'd also do it at night. A temp worker could have done it for minimum wage. He wanted work that didn't require thought. 'We have to track things,' Kim used to say.

"I said, 'Kim, you've got to stop drinking, you've got to get help. This is a problem for the company. Clean up or leave.' He left. He'd been there a few years before I confronted it. He went away briefly. Still drank. Eventually I had to lay him off anyway, in '86. Denver was going through a slump. The magazine was losing money.

"In a strange way we were the same but totally different. Our family backgrounds. We both felt our parents weren't up to the level of the people we went to school with. When you think you're meant to be more but you can't risk it . . . "

"Did Kim tell you he was ashamed of his family?" I interrupted.

"No, it's my own interpretation."

"I never sensed that Kim was ashamed of his background," I said. "If he was, he hid it well."

Garrett went on, "When you are extremely brilliant and you can do things and you don't there's a problem. Something is holding you back. If you're an intellectual, you become a Harvard professor; you don't edit articles on orchids in a shitty office next to the Regency Hotel. Kim viewed himself as very insignificant and he made himself that way. He made himself invisible. Nobody will ever know what held him back. Some people are so sensitive, their thoughts run so deep, but the world doesn't appreciate them . . . you shield yourself from the world. But Kim still had embers inside. Who knows what could have fanned them back to life?"

Kim's aunt said, "Gloria denied Kim's drinking. She protected him. She was afraid if she said anything to Kim she'd lose him."

There was a parallel here—Gloria accepting Kim's harmful behavior in order to keep him, just as Kim had accepted mine.

Seeing me out, she said, "You used to be so pretty."

I showed up at Ana Garcia's little green ranch house, next door to the Janiks' old house, unannounced. I feared she wouldn't want to talk to me if I called, feared I'd be blamed for Kim's death. Ana was now a tiny, eighty-three-year-old lady with bristly gray hair and a cane. When I said who I was, tears came to her eyes.

"Oh, honey," Ana said, "I never thought I'd see you again."

"It's been twenty-five years."

"You were so pretty then."

These mentions of my past attractiveness were getting discouraging. "I heard about Kim . . ."

"He never had another girlfriend. There was one Glorie hoped he'd marry but he said he only wanted Laurie. He didn't want anyone else. He told me you were married to a carpenter. Before that he'd say he saw you from time to time in New York; you went to plays. He still loved you, honey. It broke his heart."

"Were there any problems in the family that you knew about?" I asked.

"Oh, John put whiskey in his breakfast coffee, and early on there was some trouble with gambling. Glorie almost divorced him, but that was before they came here, a long time ago."

What? Whiskey? Gambling? I thought the Janiks had a dry house save that syrupy Mogen David wine at New Year's. Perhaps Gloria had been keeping secrets for a long time; perhaps she had other reasons to retreat into her religion besides a pact to keep John alive.

"Our kids were always in each other's houses," Ana said. "But Kim only played with Matt. Kim was always alone. Glorie and me were like this," Ana said, twining two bent fingers together, "like sisters, but she didn't tell me. I didn't know he was alcoholic, honey. Not until one night when the lights were out over there, Glorie called to ask if we had lights. Then I saw her out at the back, looking through the sliding doors. She was looking for Kim. He was hiding out back. The next morning my neighbor across the street called and asked what was going on. She saw the police talking to Kim last night. I found out he went after Glorie with a screwdriver. She called the cops. They put him in a what do you call it?"

"A detox?"

"Yes. A detox. He got out two days later and Glorie had taken all his liquor bottles out of his suitcase. She broke them and poured them out. When Kim got back he was so mad, honey! He yelled at her and took off. He didn't say goodbye. She went somewhere and when she got back, he was gone. She died after that and Kim came right away. When they were burying the ashes, Kim slipped in the hole."

"Oh my God, was he drunk?" I asked.

"No," Ana said.

Carla, Ana's beautiful, overweight, thirteen-year-old granddaughter, said from the kitchen, "I think he was."

"When he fell in," Ana continued, "Sue said, 'Come back, Kim, it's not your time yet.' Kim never got to say goodbye to his mother. I think the guilt, you know, was awful. He used to come in the summers. He cooked for her when she came home from work. Or they cooked together. Kim chopping over here, Glorie over there—together. He'd say, 'Come on, Ana, we're going out,' and he'd take me and Glorie for dinner."

Carla came into the room. She said, "One night he called my mom at 3:00 A.M. and said, 'They're after me.' But we couldn't understand what he was saying. Two weeks later he was dead."

Ana said, "July 11, the day he died, I woke up and saw a light and someone standing there—I couldn't see his face. After that we found out about him dying. It was so awful, Laurie. I think of the animals eating him."

Before I left, Ana asked if I had a picture of my child. I pulled out the only snapshot I had with me, an old one, Becky a toddler hanging over Tom's shoulder. "She looks like her daddy," I said, "with those curls." I felt uneasy showing the picture, wondering if Ana thought I should have had Kim's child instead.

As I was leaving, Ana said, "I always watered from their well. The new neighbors won't share their water. I wish Matt would talk to them about it."

You look for reasons, want to reduce it down to something understandable. Kim's family blamed the alcohol alone for his demise. Of course, it does alter the brain and change the personality, just as it dissolves the calcium in bones and leaves the alcoholic fragile, prone to breakage. I have to factor in the unhappy circumstance of Kim being a sensitive, bright misfit in a rough small town, the child of a Jehovah's Witness, a nearly friendless fat kid who had tried to buy buddies with candy from his grandfather's garage.

Recently I read the catalog of a posthumous exhibit of paintings by an artist I knew in New York. Robert nearly killed himself with a four-gram-a-day cocaine habit, got clean, came out as gay, and died of AIDS. Robert's last years were lived mostly in isolation, in his studio, where he tried to make some visual, emotional sense of the knowledge that his body was ravaged, that he wouldn't have enough time, that he would die young. In an interview, Robert said, "As long as I can remember, I always felt different from others. . . . I never got used to the ridicule I experienced on a daily basis during my adolescence in school. It always caught me by surprise and made me feel tremendous shame and loneliness." Reading Robert's words, I thought of Kim.

I have to factor in Harvard, where, instead of finding a true home, Kim met a whole new form of exclusion. And then, of course, there was me. When I think about our history together, I see that from the time that we first put out our thumbs on a highway in 1971 until he came east to visit me at college in 1973, Kim was altered permanently. There's no way around the fact that it was in response to me. Sure, the times affected him—the questioning of institutions and authorities, waiting to be drafted, the counterculture chaos, drugs. But none of that changed his essential core as did his growing mistrust of and disappointment in me, which coexisted with his determination to love me at any cost.

I question my narcissism here once again. Sure, it's possible that he was bent on being the loner he became, the isolate, and his Harvard friends and devotion to me were an aberration that, in the long run, wouldn't determine the shape his life took. But I don't believe it. Whatever his propensities, I saw him transformed. The man who said he'd never opened himself to anyone before became the man certain he could live off his own flesh.

In 1973 he wrote me, referring to Alyosha Karamazov's devil, that men long for disturbance, and that through the ministrations of the devil alone do they truly feel their lives. The devil, he said, waits for saints to fall into depravity. I was the devil Kim longed for and he fell.

I'm afraid that someone reading this will think Kim a pathetic fool for loving me, for giving me so much rope with which to hang him. I too interpreted his tolerance as weakness and felt the fearful power of a child whose parents cannot set limits. But I wonder if Kim also saw beyond my floundering, beyond behavior that would now be labeled symptomatic. Perhaps he focused on the nearly invisible nub of decency, clarity, and sense that eventually allowed me to be a tender mother to my child, a faithful wife. He insisted on believing in a worthwhile Laurie long before I saw a glimpse of her, long before I had any faith. Does it count that I am thankful now? Or did his steadfastness only further encourage my outrages?

Nearly everyone I spoke to acknowledged that they didn't really know Kim. His brother, roommate, employers, neighbors, relatives. He was a person who didn't allow himself to be known. But there were years when he felt I knew him, when he wanted me to know him, when he laid out his dreams and ideas and fears for me in tales and letters and poems. "Here's one I think you'll like," he'd say. And I was too young, too damaged, and then too hungry for the rest of the world to value what he offered. At twenty he believed he'd found a soul mate, and as far as I know he never felt that way, never tried to feel that way, with anyone else. That he was so injured by his love for me was our mutual failing—his addictiveness was evident long before the alcohol took hold. There was a key-in-the-lock, tumblers-lining-up click to the way we were drawn together, first by admiration, later by needs so visceral and hidden even we couldn't decipher them.

Tom said, "You've made me feel that Kim mattered. That something was really lost when he died." I'm grateful for his willingness to change opinions, to put defensiveness aside, to grant Kim the status of a complex person, not just a sad drunk wallowing in his past "glory days." I wonder if Tom is able to see Kim—even this distilled and partial version—more wholly than I can.

"You must feel freed now," Tom said, "purged of all this."

But I don't. There's no freedom in the knowledge of how Kim died or in forcing myself to admit the role I played in his misery. Nothing has been exorcised, nothing transcended. The past keeps surfacing and surfacing.

Tom's great joy is bringing back overgrown forest to the fields once created by eighteenth-century farmers, men who ruptured themselves digging stumps, hauling stones, making these walls that ring our house and now run through forest instead of field. He burns brush, clears, clears. I wanted to do that with Kim's story, our story, clear away the shrubby growth, the confusions of time and memory, make sense and order. I wanted Kim's life to add up to more than a broken plastic flowerpot beside an unmarked grave.

Perhaps it always has. Who knows how many thousands of students he taught to think clearly, how many writers he helped? Nearly everyone remarked on his kindness. He is irrevocably in me, and I'm still here.

At age twenty Kim wrote:

> Amid the phantom cries of charioteers
> Agony of men and horses echoing in the emptiness
> The sole remnant of beauty lies: the rubble of Troy.
> Unknown beneath the fallen stone
> The dead are spared a death that fades
> The withered face of Helen's age.

Kim knew so much more than he could live. And he was spared the withering of his immense, illusory love. At twenty-two, I sat in my brother's car at dawn outside a bus station. Windshield wipers sluiced glass, and light reflected in puddles. I put my hands to my face and felt, through rubbery warm skin, the shocking fact of my face stripped to grinning skull: a quick glimpse past my own existence. At thirty I rode a clacking New York subway under advertisements for hemorrhoid remedies and roach poison and thought, *I've been young for so long. It seems like forever.* Then I realized, if I lived, I'd be old for much longer. I am older now than Kim was when he died.

On the last day of my Colorado trip I drove the rental car up to southeast Wyoming, near the Colorado and Nebraska borders, to Hawk Springs. I had the idea that I might find a piece of Kim, something I'd missed, by seeing what he'd seen in his last hours. Sustained, low-level panic accompanied me much of the way. The landscape slid by—great alternating fields of furrowed brown and planted green. I cruised through a patchwork like the ones I've viewed from airplanes. An uncommon number of motorcycles roared by me on the two-lane highway. The sun shone perfectly bright, and wind blew the grasses. When I found the turnoff, a new fear surfaced: the dirt road was rutted and muddy; there had been monsoon rains recently, as when Kim got his car stuck. I was afraid I'd get stuck too.

Hawk Springs State Recreation Area looked harmless—an oasis of cottonwood and willow ringing a large man-made lake damned at the near end. There were campsites, restrooms, a kids' play yard. "Don't take my butt," a woman washing her hair under an outdoor spigot warned a man who pointed a camera. RVs settled into their slots, towing small cars or skiffs, heaped with bikes, gas grills, lawn chairs. Kids' voices shrilled from a swing set and climber. An official sign listed regulations about the kinds of fish in the lake: dace, bass, perch, trout. A lawnmower buzzed. The water rippled and sparkled under high clouds, its surface evaporating under the empty blue sky.

The man mowing the grass turned off his machine and removed his ear protectors when I approached. I asked if he knew anything about Kim's death here two years ago. He didn't. He warned me to look out for rattlers and bull snakes when I said that I was going to cross the dam.

Beyond the parking area, the grassy, banked dam was gated. Kim had removed the gate, despite the No Trespassing sign. He preferred to break down a gate rather than camp near tourists, risk having to talk to anyone, or perhaps having them observe his peculiar solitude.

A snake wriggled past my boots in the rough weeds of the dam crossing. I opted to walk a muddy dirt two-track that ran below the dam. The lower road passed by a bubbling spring and bellowing Herefords, wild sunflowers as plentiful as in Arles. Barbed wire fences ran through grass and sage. I was relieved that Kim had died in a place this beautiful. I had pictured parched earth, dust, a New Mexico landscape instead of this lush green garden.

The road looped away and, some distance later, swung back toward the lake. A deer leaped out of the brush then stood for a long time in front of me, not more than thirty feet away. I spoke to it, feeling spooked and blessed. The animal bounded away.

In a tangle of cottonwoods just beyond the far end of the dam, a couple of boarded up trailers propped with cement blocks, some slapped together plywood furniture, gave the look of semipermanence that says locals camp here. Kim was headed for this side.

I followed various paths and muddy truck ruts for a long time, wondering if I was on the one he'd followed. Why hadn't he returned to the recreation area for help? Of course, Kim never asked anyone for help. Why hadn't he at least walked back on the road he drove in on? Matt said Kim had made it most of the three miles to the highway. He knew where he was going; he just couldn't get there.

After two hours of futile searching I gave up. It was impossible to know exactly where Kim had collapsed without dragging Matt up here or finding the right local cop. And what did it matter, after all? Kim was no more here, where his spirit had left him, than in the Morrissey cemetery or in Minturn, where the Eagle River ran and ran.

Walking back, I plucked wildflowers and sage blossoms. I pocketed a small rusty stone with a raised white circle and a flat piece of beat-up metal shaped like a mushroom that might have been a belt buckle or a car part. In the absence of an apparition, I needed something tangible to hold.

The tires whirl hopelessly, a spinning whine. He's got a headache already and now this. He rocks it back and forth, accelerator, brakes, but she won't pop free. He tries to push, one hand on the steering wheel, one on the doorframe, his sneakers sliding in muck. No go. He pulls a shirt, a sweatshirt, an extra pair of jeans from the trunk and stuffs them under the tires as best he can. When he kneels before the tires, his hip aches. Sweat runs down his chest, down his sides, prickling. His breath is short. He gets back in the Saturn and tries again—accelerator, brake—*Damn.*

The sun beats down mercilessly. Kim puts on the blue Rockies cap, locks the car, starts walking. If he cuts across the open land he can make it to the road in about an hour, then hitch a ride to the nearest town and hire a wrecker to pull him out. It will be a hassle because he's taken the gate down illegally and the last thing he needs is some-one asking for his license.

He's thirsty. It will probably be three hours before he gets the car unstuck, and another hour to set up camp before he can start fish-ing. His head pounds like a jackhammer. His hip aches. His arms feel shaky. He's so thirsty. Damn the sunflowers waving in the parching wind. It's hot, too hot. He'll just sit for a moment and rest. Now his heartbeat keeps rhythm with the pound in his head. Grasshoppers rustle in the weeds; birds fly up. If he had the energy he'd fill his hat with grasshoppers for bait.

He looks at the sky: the sun has spread into a pale that pulses. He wills it to disappear. At Harvard there was a solar eclipse. They went out to the crowded Quincy House courtyard. Kids were holding up smoked glass, X ray film. He borrowed a piece for Laurie. From across the quad music blasted: *Little darling, I see the ice is slowly melting . . . it seems like years since you've been here . . . Here comes the sun . . .*

The goddamn sun. He better get going. It must be over a hundred. A hot wind blows the grasses flat. He can feel it sucking the mois-ture out of his cells, turning him into paper, a cascade of paper, all the pages he's written, the pages he's read. He imagines this blister-ing wind tearing them from him like a calendar in an old-time mov-ie. Leaving a husk.

They husked the corn they stole from old Jim's garden in the emp-ty lot. Jim lived on carrots all winter and turned orange. The carrots hurt his liver. The doctors said your liver is swollen you're dehydrat-ed you need an IV we can't be responsible . . . He's heard it all be-fore. He just needs to sit again, for a little while. This will take lon-ger than he expected. He wants to be standing in the shade of the cottonwoods on the lake edge, casting his line, reeling, but he kneels and heaves. There's nothing in him to give up and the spasms wrack his bones. He'll just lie here for a while, wait for the pounding to stop. Get his strength back. He's got to get moving. Tonight he'll be fish-ing under the cottonwoods.

Dad says, "Keep the tension on the reel, don't let it out yet, not yet, not yet . . ." The line slips through Kim's fingers and he's sorry. He's going to go fishing on the Cache La Poudre River someday. He's always meant to. Water tumbling over mountain boulders, a spume of spray, his sneakers wet, the branches leaning over in a bower.

Her hair falls like dark water but when she laughs, her coldness makes his skin shiver. He's freezing. Later he's so hot he whips his shirt off, and his wallet spills from his jeans, and he's barefoot in the prickers but the grass is soft under his feet because Dad has his own well, and he waters every day. Kim doesn't need shoes, so he kicks them off, and the grass between his toes tickles.

His mother tickles, tickles, he's on her lap laughing, laughing with her face above him.

"John Kim, John Kim." She walks beside him.

"I'm sorry," Kim tells his mother. "I didn't mean it."

She loads his arms with copies of *The Watchtower,* thin paper with gaudy black and white drawings of religious ecstasy and damnation: the second coming, a robed man hunched forward in a posture of terror as God breaks through the clouds. The clouds stack up like that over Mount Arapaho beyond their backyard. A landscape that lends itself to images of splendor and devastation.

Kim closes his eyes against the sun's glare, imagines himself home, touching a finger to the soil in his African violets, testing the dampness. He hopes Mr. Jensen will take him up in the hills again this weekend looking for specimens, naming the flowers, and afterward he will sit and study their parts, turning the knob on the microscope. He wishes he had an instrument so powerful he could keep turning until the smallest parts were revealed in their patterns. *You are an instrument of the Lord,* she said. Would he burn in hell for worshipping another hierarchy, not his mother's angels and saints and Jehovah, but the order of molecules and atoms, the constancy of planets revolving in their spheres?

"I'll never stop praying for you," she says. "I'll walk beside you John Kim, me and Jesus."

I believe in the rational mind.

Jesus.

about suffering they were never wrong the old masters . . .

Are you an English major? I'm only in eleventh grade.

The ship rolls. The jet wheels and tumbles, he pukes in his oxygen mask, the stars whirl above. He wakes to freezing darkness. He never knew it would look like this, knees to chin in the tiny cockpit, the blue Earth spinning below. The sky glitters and everything rushes toward him.

If this were fiction perhaps I'd write it like that. I'd say I could know him only by inhabiting him, by taking possession of his mind as I took possession of his soul. But it would be a lie. I'd supplant the real Kim with the one I'd invented. Maybe I have, despite my efforts to find the truth here. Perhaps he's eluded me as he eluded everyone else. What I don't know of Kim's death—and his life—could fill that vast blue sky over the reservoir.

I don't know what happened in those barrooms, with those lovers, in those crashed cars, the fields he woke up in, the times he called to me, cursed me, imagined me. I don't even have his notebooks. I know he died naked, curled into a fetal ball. Did he call for me, or for his mother, or even, at last, for Jesus? Did he welcome surrender? Was he afraid? Did he take comfort in his own insignificance beside this prehistoric ocean, this sea of grass?

> *January 26, 1988, a dream:*
>
> *I was with Tom and Becky and my parents, and Kim's body. Kim was young, in his familiar blue jeans and light blue button-down shirt, his hair blond and a little long. But he was dead, and we needed to do something with his body. It seemed like days were passing while I kept changing clothes, trying to find something that I didn't look too fat in. There was the body, laid out on a bed, laid out on the floor, unchanging. We were in some kind of a hotel, and behind it was the crematorium and the cemetery where his parents were buried. I thought we'd had the body too long, and it would soon rot. I wanted to put it into a casket and have it cremated, but we needed to leave. I was afraid they wouldn't really bury Kim, just throw out his ashes, if we took off. His body had finally stiffened. It wouldn't go in the casket—one arm stuck out. I had to leave but I wanted to save a bone from the ashes, a small piece to take with me.*

My daughter's seventh birthday. After supper and the carrot cake she requested, the spitty blowing out of the candles, we take a walk through the wooded hills behind our house, all of us fanned out: Tom in the lead, Becky and I, her new birthday puppy she's named Lizzy floundering along through brush and prickers and downed branches. Our grown dog scouts left and right, nose to the ground, following deer trails, and even the smoke gray cat follows. We are not long past the switch to Daylight Savings and we're all a bit drunk on the novelty of evening light. April, and we know how short this easy walking season is: we are poised between snowmelt and black fly season, those tiny, vicious biters that leave welts.

"What tree does black birch like to live near?" Tom quizzes Becky.

"I know," she says, "but I can't think of its name." She waves a needled branch to demonstrate.

"Right," says Tom. "Hemlock."

Becky and I stop to sit on a rocky crag. She leans against my knees. With the trees still leafless we can see, through branches, sunlit hilltops, orchards and fields, and the glint from a window in a new software mansion across the river in New Hampshire. Tom has picked up two short thick sticks and knocks them together as he walks, a hollow rhythmic tolling, drawing us from our perch as if he were some sawdust-laden Pied Piper.

Here are ledge, quartz, fern, moss, tumbled walls that mark our land. Above me, bare branches still scrape and yearn skyward. The puppy struggles to keep up. We are her pack now. I think again of a twenty-year-old Kim's words about not being able to remain downhearted when he sat alone by the ocean; his own insignificance reassured him. But there is no refuge in insignificance, just as there is none in prominence. There is only this.